STAR STRUCK QUILTS

Dazzling Diamonds & Traditional Blocks

13 Skill-Building Projects

Barbara H. Cline

C&T PUBLISHING

Text copyright © 2010 by Barbara H. Cline

Artwork copyright © 2010 by C&T Publishing, Inc.

Publisher: Amy Marson

Creative Director: Gailen Runge

Acquisitions Editor: Susanne Woods

Editor: Cynthia Bix

Technical Editors: Susan Nelsen and Joyce Lytle

Copyeditor/Proofreader: Wordfirm Inc.

Cover Designer: Kristy Zacharias

Book Designer: Christina D. Jarumay

Production Coordinator: Jenny Leicester

Production Editor: Alice Mace Nakanishi

Illustrator: Wendy Mathson

Photography by Christina Carty-Francis and Diane Pedersen of C&T Publishing, Inc., unless otherwise noted

Published by C&T Publishing, Inc., P.O. Box 1456, Lafayette, CA 94549

Library of Congress Cataloging-in-Publication Data

Cline, Barbara H.

 Star struck quilts : dazzling diamonds & traditional blocks : 13 skill-building projects / by Barbara H. Cline.

  p. cm.

 ISBN 978-1-57120-959-7 (soft cover)

 1. Patchwork--Patterns. 2. Quilting--Patterns. I. Title.

 TT835.C596 2010

 746.46'041--dc22

                                2009051361

Printed in China

10 9 8 7 6 5 4 3 2 1

ACKNOWLEDGMENTS

Thanks to my husband
and children, who have been a
real support and encouragement
to me by being my cheerleaders
as well as my critics.

To my sisters, who have inspired me
in the quilting world and challenged me
to try new and different avenues of quilting.

To all of the quilters in my classes,
for sharing their love and joy of quilting with me.

To Joyce Horst, who helped me write my "Life Lessons."

And to everyone at C&T Publishing—Cynthia Bix, Christina Jarumay,
Jenny Leicester, Susan Nelsen, Gailen Runge, and Susanne Woods.

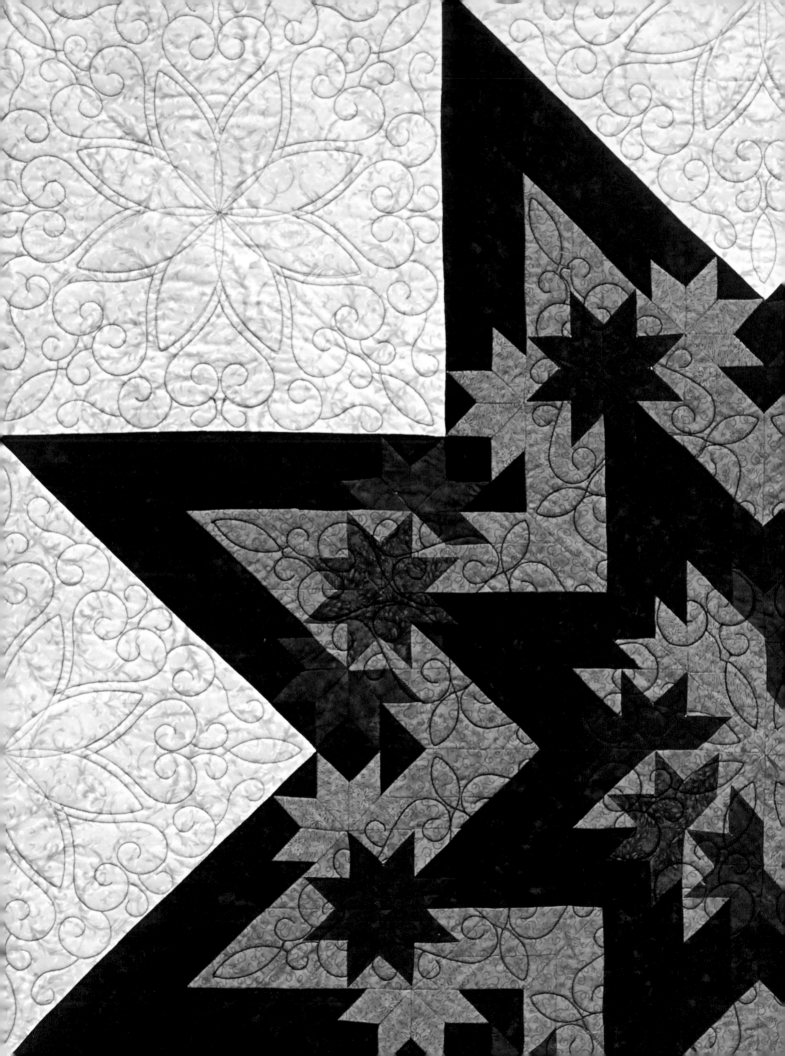

CONTENTS

INTRODUCTION

Blazing Star, 48″ × 48″, made and machine quilted by Barbara Cline (project on page 52)

The Lone Star quilt pattern is one of the oldest, most recognized patterns in American culture. Basically, it is an eight-pointed star composed of diamond shapes that can be laid out in a variety of ways to create new eye-catching designs. Through the years, various arrangements of the Lone Star pattern have taken on new names, including Blazing Star, Rising Star, Touching Star, and Broken Star. In the Native American culture, this pattern is known as the Morning Star.

In this book, you will learn simple secrets for sewing Lone Star layouts. You'll discover how to create diamonds more easily than ever, using rotary cutting and strip piecing. This book features nine stars that can stand alone or can be set into larger quilt settings. If you wished, you could create 27 different star quilts! The mix-and-match patterns will inspire you and give you new ideas. Before long, you will be sewing complex stars that sparkle.

In the first section of the book—Lone Star Basics—you will learn the basics of Lone Star layouts and of piecing diamonds. This is not a beginner's quilt; in fact, if it's not done properly, the finished quilt will not lie flat, or the eight points will not meet in the center. This first section contains tips and tricks to help you avoid these problems.

In the next section—Star Quilts: Simple to Complex—you will find patterns for nine Lone Star wall quilts that will challenge you to go beyond your limits. The projects start with a basic large Lone Star. The next star includes a more complex design, and the next a design even more complex than the last. Each star will challenge you in a new way as different concepts are introduced. Each step-by-step pattern will become more challenging as the piecing becomes increasingly intricate. Concepts introduced include choosing fabrics, fussy cutting diamonds, piecing borders behind the main star, strip piecing with diamonds, and machine appliquéing.

The last section—Create Your Own Quilt—includes a variety of ways in which the Lone Stars can be sewn into larger quilt layouts. Mix and match to combine various designs into your own personal design. Unlock the creativity in your own heart and mind.

The final project in this section uses the striking Midnight Star as a dynamic center for a challenging background of advanced Diamond Chain blocks—the ultimate challenge for this collection of Lone Star beauties.

Along with the quilt patterns, I offer my own "Life Lessons." I grew up in the Shenandoah Valley of Virginia, in a close-knit Mennonite family, where sewing and quilting were entwined into our everyday lives. These are stories of happenings in my life from which I learned valuable lessons that I apply to my life today. I hope you enjoy them and can learn something from my experiences.

This is a wall quilt I pieced from a photograph of my grandmother, Vera Heatwole. She taught all of her daughters and many of her granddaughters how to quilt. Her love of sewing and quilting has been passed on to the following generations.

LONE STAR

BASICS

Summer Night Twinkle Star, 48″ × 48″, made and machine quilted by Barbara Cline

In this section, you'll learn about the many ways in which the stars and their basic diamond units can be put together, as well as some basics about color, fabric preparation, and supplies you'll need. Here you'll also find instruction in basic techniques that will help you construct perfect stars.

LONE STAR LAYOUTS

Lone Star quilts feature eight-pointed stars composed of diamond shapes laid out in a variety of designs and combinations. Most commonly, they are laid out so that they seem to form rings of different colors radiating out from the center. The Lone Stars in this book are made up of diamonds (actually parallelograms) that have two 45° angles and two 135° angles.

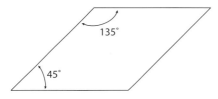

The number of smaller diamonds in a diamond layout determines the quilt's dimensions, as well as the way in which each diamond is pieced and colored to create designs within the layout. In a traditional Lone Star, the center star is one color, the next row of diamonds circling the center star is another color, the next another, and so on, out to the tips of the star points.

Choosing Color

Value plays a very important role when choosing colors for these layouts. Value refers to the lightness or darkness of a color. Below is an example with grays. Squint your eyes and hold the book at arm's length to see the light, medium, and dark values.

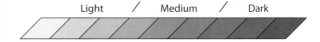

For the designs to be effective, you need value contrast among the fabrics used to create the diamonds. To check that I have enough difference in value between two fabrics, I squint my eyes and stand about nine feet from the fabrics. Then I ask myself, "Do I see two distinct colors, or do they blend together and look like one color?" The goal is to see two distinct colors. I often use this method when picking out fabrics for customers at the fabric store where I work.

You will learn more about fabric color in the quilt project instructions for *Star Tricks* (page 38), *Midnight Star* (page 48), *Blazing Star* (page 52), and *Ivy Spangled Banner* (page 58).

Different arrangements of colors in the diamonds will create different designs within the layout.

Diamond Layouts

The Lone Star's diamond layout is made of eight *large diamonds,* and each large diamond is made of smaller diamonds called *diamond units.* These diamond units often contain other diamonds and shapes. The *background* comprises triangles and squares that are added around the Lone Star to make a square.

The number of diamond units that make up a large diamond can vary. The layouts are expressed in terms of rows—for example, 2 × 2 indicates 2 rows of 2 diamond units each. A large diamond can have as few as 2 rows and as many as 15 rows or even more.

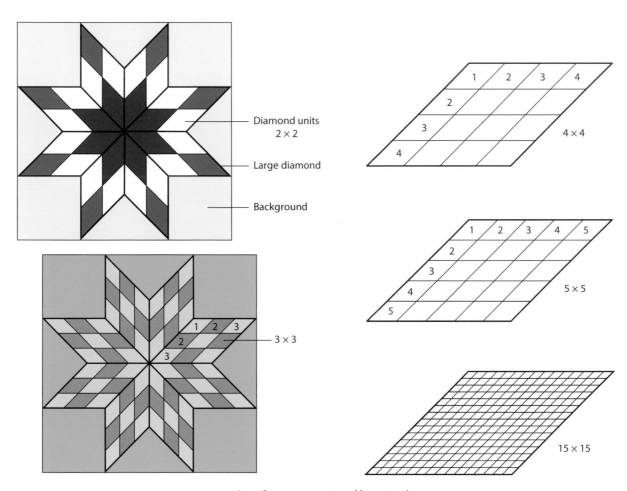

Diamond units
2 × 2

Large diamond

Background

4 × 4

3 × 3

5 × 5

15 × 15

Lone Star components and layout options

Pieced diamond units can add dimension and color to a traditional Lone Star design of one-patch diamond units. To illustrate my point, let's take a traditional Lone Star layout made up of one-patch diamond units and substitute pieced diamond units for some of the one-patches. Notice that in this example, the background of the pieced diamond units is the same as the color of the original one-patches. In some cases, however, there will not be any Lone Star color in the diamond unit. By adding the pieced diamond unit, the pattern moves from the traditional to the nontraditional Lone Star.

Traditional Lone Star

Pieced diamond unit to be placed inside traditional Lone Star

The two combined

Traditional Lone Star designs, such as *Gradient Star* (page 26), feature large diamonds made of simple one-patch diamond units. Nontraditional Lone Star designs include diamond units pieced from two or more different fabrics in a variety of ways, from simple halves or quarters to more complex designs.

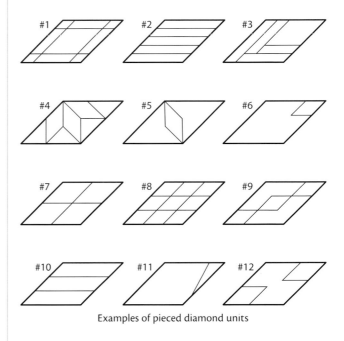

Examples of pieced diamond units

As you become more experienced in making these quilts, you can be creative with your ideas. Use paper and colored pencils to design different diamonds and place them in a diamond layout. The following quilts have a few examples of diamond layouts that use different styles of diamond units. Look carefully at the quilts close-up to analyze the use of nontraditional elements.

Patchwork Spins, 48" × 48", made and machine quilted by Barbara Cline

Patchwork Spins diamond units

Summer Night Twinkle Star (detail below) contains examples of five pieced diamond units, as well as diamond units that are not broken down.

Summer Night Twinkle Star diamond units (full quilt on page 8)

Whirling Stars, 60″ × 60″, made and machine quilted by Barbara Cline

Whirling Stars shows further use of nontraditional diamond units to create a spinning array of stars, with the Lone Star as the background. Each star was cut using a stack and cut method.

Whirling Stars diamond units

Star Tricks, 48″ × 48″, made and machine quilted by Barbara Cline

Piecing the background pieces adds another dimension to the Lone Star layout. This allows the design to move outside the diamond layout, enhancing the background and creating a completely different look. The background of the traditional layout consists of four triangles and four squares. If you look at *Star Tricks*, you can see that the four background squares are broken down (see project on page 38). Each square is divided into two triangles. One of those triangles is then broken into two diamonds and three triangles, and those diamonds are broken further into strips. This large broken triangle is also used as the background side triangle.

Another example of putting design in the background triangles and squares can be seen in *Star Ripple* (page 43). In this quilt, diamonds are appliquéd on top of the background units of squares and triangles, making it look like the star is placed on top of the circle of diamonds.

In the projects *Star Reflections* (page 34) and *Blazing Star* (page 52), you will learn how to make borders that create a still different effect. As you can see, you can change the design in a variety of ways by breaking down each diamond into diamond units, working with different colors in the diamond layout, changing the diamond units, working outside the diamond layout, and changing the background design. In Create Your Own Quilt (page 71), you will learn how to add blocks around a diamond layout to make a full-size quilt.

WHAT YOU NEED TO KNOW

You'll need to use the following supplies and techniques to make the quilt projects in this book.

Supplies

You need only basic quilting supplies to make these quilts. The following are the supplies I recommend.

- **Rotary cutter,** with a sharp new blade

- **Rotary cutting mat,** 24″ × 36″

- **Rotary cutting rulers,** 6″ × 24 and 4″ × 14″—The smaller ruler is not so clumsy and is easier to handle when cutting strips into diamonds.

- **Pins**—I like the Nifty Notions Flower Head Pins. At 2″ long and .05mm, they are thin, long, and easy to pick up.

- **Sewing thread** to match fabric—You may need a couple of different colors for each quilt.

- **¼″-wide presser foot** for your sewing machine—Check to make sure it is accurate.

- **Scissors** for clipping threads and trimming dog ears

- **Seam ripper**

- **Template plastic**

- **Iron and ironing board**

- **Spray starch**—I like Best Press (Mary Ellen's) because it doesn't have a lot of sizing—it doesn't make the fabric too stiff, but it does provide enough stability to keep the fabric from stretching.

- **Retayne** (G&K Craft Industries), *optional*—You can add this in your washing machine to keep fabrics from bleeding.

- **Perfect Piecer** (Jinny Beyer)—This tool has different angles to mark the ¼″ dots that are crucial for the pieces joined in a Y-seam.

- **Pen-style Chaco liner** (Clover)—This marker is great for marking pattern pieces.

Fabric Preparation and Pressing

I prefer to preshrink my fabrics. First of all, because darker fabrics tend to bleed, I add Retayne to the washing machine when preshrinking to keep the fabrics from bleeding. Second, some fabrics shrink more than others. If you don't preshrink the fabrics, they might shrink to different sizes after the quilt is pieced and washed, which means the finished quilt may not lie flat.

As you cut the diamond shapes, at least some of the edges will be cut on the bias. To keep these edges from stretching and distorting, handle the diamonds as little as possible, and use spray starch to keep the fabric from stretching. Before cutting the fabric, spray it lightly with Best Press, and press till dry. Once the large diamonds are made, blocking the diamonds helps ensure the proper size and shape for the diamonds (page 22).

Throughout the instructions, you will be told which way the seams should be pressed. Follow the pressing arrows so that the seams will nest together. After each sewing step, I press without steam until I have sewn a completed block or diamond; then I use steam.

Creating Large Diamonds

The diamond units that make up the large diamonds may be created in one of two ways: (1) by cutting them out individually in the traditional way with diamond-shaped templates, particularly used for fussy cutting, or (2) by cutting them from strips of fabric in a strip set or from individual fabric strips.

INDIVIDUAL DIAMONDS CUT WITH TEMPLATES

Cutting diamonds with templates is the best method to use when you want to fussy cut. Fussy cutting means zeroing in on a fabric design or motif when you cut the fabric. When you fussy cut, all the edges may be bias, so you must be careful to keep the fabric from stretching.

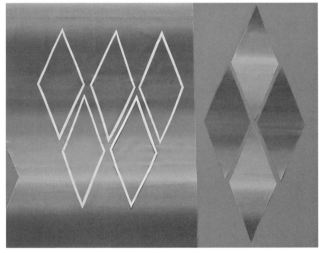

Fussy cutting

To make your own templates, use template plastic, which is available at your local quilt store. If a project calls for a template to be made, specific measurements will be given in the instructions for drawing the template on the template plastic with a fine-tipped marker. Cut out the template, being careful to cut right in the center of the lines, not to the right or left of them. Add a grainline as indicated in the project instructions.

When you cut the fabric, you will be dealing with bias edges, so spray the fabric first with spray starch (page 15). The diagrams show which cuts are on the bias. Depending on the placement of the grainline, the diamonds may have two or four bias edges. Fussy-cut diamonds may have no regard for the grainline at all, since you are using very specific motifs in the fabric for the diamonds.

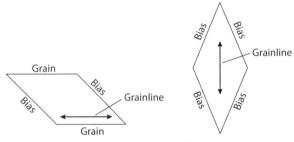

Templates with grainlines

Once I have the template, I position it on the desired fabric motif. I do not mark the fabric. I actually cut the fabric right around the template plastic with my rotary cutter. In class, sometimes I have a student lay a ruler over the top of the template plastic to help cut around the template. Drawing around the template would be a great idea for beginners who might shave off the edges of their templates.

DIAMONDS CUT FROM STRIPS AND STRIP SETS

Years before rotary mats, rulers, and cutters were invented, these quilts were made using cardboard diamond patterns, with each diamond cut out individually and then pieced. This process required many little tedious cuts and was very time consuming. In addition, the cardboard patterns would wear down, leading to distorted diamond patterns that resulted in inaccurate piecing. Strip piecing has made diamond quilts so much easier and quicker! We have greater accuracy and speed, thanks to modern rotary tools and supplies.

STAR STRUCK QUILTS

CUTTING EQUILATERAL DIAMONDS

An equilateral diamond is created when the strip width is the same as the diamond width in the cutting instructions. If the instructions say to "cut diamonds," the diamonds are equilateral. The width of each diamond equals the strip width. When cutting equilateral diamonds, you may want to fold the strip in half so that you can cut more than one diamond at a time.

Equilateral diamond

1. For all the diamonds in this book, your cuts will be at a 45° angle. To achieve this angle, place the strip parallel to the bottom edge of the cutting mat, lining up the edge on a horizontal grid line. Place the ruler on top of the fabric, aligning the ruler's 45° line with the horizontal edge of the cut strip. Cut on this angle. This initial cut will create the first edge of the diamond.

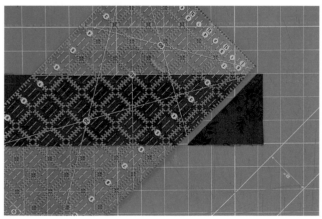

45° angle cut on single strip

2. Refer to the instructions for the desired diamond width. Use a ruler to measure *the width from the first cut edge,* keeping the ruler at the same 45° angle. Make the next cut. Repeat along the length of the strip to make the number of cuts required for the project.

Cutting diamonds from single strip

CUTTING LONG DIAMONDS

When you are rotary cutting single diamonds and diamond strips that are not equilateral, you will cut either to the upper right or to the upper left, depending on the project instructions. Each cutting direction produces a unique diamond, and it is important to keep the terms distinct: Diagonal cuts to the right produce right long diamonds. *Diagonal cuts to the left produce* left long diamonds. *The illustration shows the two types of long diamonds. In all long diamond subcutting, the right side of the fabric must always be facing up. If you wish, you can stack the strips and cut double fabric layers, but never fold these strips.*

Long right diamond   Long left diamond

Creating a strip set

In some projects, you will create strip sets to speed up the diamond cutting process. Specific information about the numbers of strips and their widths will be given in the project instructions, but here are some strip set basics for your reference.

- Always place the fabric faceup to cut on the mat.

- As you arrange the strip set, offset the strips by the width of the strip.

- The order and direction in which you arrange and sew the strips will determine the pattern.

- All the diamonds and diamond strips in this book are cut at a 45° angle.

The following is only an example of a strip set. A particular project may have you arranging the strips as stairsteps in the opposite direction. Each project will have specific instructions and illustrations for the strip sets and the direction of the cuts.

1. Place strip 1 on your cutting mat, right side up.

2. Place strip 2 beneath strip 1. Offset the left edge of this strip by the width of the strip as shown. Repeat for strips 3–5.

Strip 1
Strip 2
Strip 3
Strip 4
Strip 5

3. Pin and sew the strips together in their proper order. To keep the strips from curving, sew the seams in alternating directions, and let the sewing machine do the work. Do not pull on the fabric strips as you sew. Press the seams in the direction indicated in the project instructions.

Rotary cutting diamond strips and sewing rows together

1. For all the diamond strips in this book, your cuts will be at a 45° angle. To achieve this angle, place the strip or strip set parallel to the bottom edge of the cutting mat, lining up the edge on a horizontal grid line. Place the ruler on top of the fabric, aligning the ruler's 45° line with the horizontal edge of the cut strip. This initial cut will create the first edge of the diamond or diamond strip.

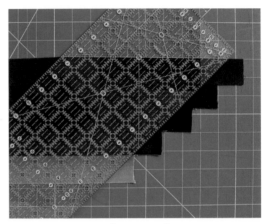

45° angle cut on strip set

2. Refer to the project instructions for the desired strip set width. Use a ruler to measure the width from the first cut edge, keeping the ruler at the same 45° angle. Make the next cut. Repeat along the length of the strip set to make the number of cuts required for the project.

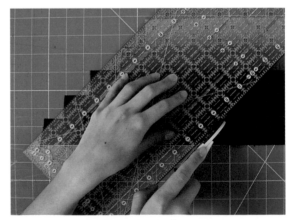

Cutting diamond strips from strip set

3. To join 2 diamond strips, place strips right sides together. Align each seam of the strip, and secure with pins. Then sew the seam. Check for seam alignment before pressing the seam.

tip

PINNING THE SEAMS

To sew 2 diamond strips together accurately, pinning is critical. With right sides together, align the seams of the 2 strips. From the wrong side of the first strip, insert a pin through the first seam ¼" from the fabric edge. Now push the tip of the same pin into the matching seam of the second strip ¼" from the fabric edge. As you slide the 2 diamonds together on the pin, the seams should be perfectly matched. Once you have sewn the seam, open it up to check.

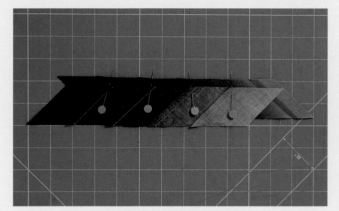

Place fabric right sides together.

Essential Techniques

The techniques presented in this section—sewing Y-seams, blocking, assembling the star, and mitering borders—are essential for creating a star quilt top that lies flat when finished and that has points that come together properly in the center.

Y-SEAMS

The Y-seam, also called a set-in seam, is required for sewing three pieces of fabric that come together to create a Y. Throughout this book, you will be working with Y-seams, which have one 90° angle and two 135° angles. Each quilt in this book has Y-seams in the large diamond layouts and sometimes in the diamond units.

A completed Y-seam has three seams, joining three sections together. The stitching of all three seams meets together at the same point. This point must be marked exactly with a dot ¼" from the cut edges of each fabric section. The stitching for each seam starts or stops at these dots.

Note the dots on each section in the diagram. All Y-seams are sewn in the same order: the sides of the Y are sewn first, and the leg of the Y is sewn last. The dots, the order number for the seams, and the stitching lines are all indicated in the Y-seam diagram.

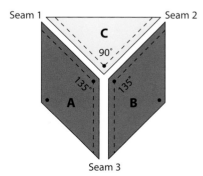

Always start or stop at dot.

Constructing the Y–seam

1. Lay out the A, B, and C pieces needed for sewing the Y-seam. With a fabric marker, mark the fabric with corresponding dots ¼″ in from where the center of the Y-seam will meet on each piece. I use the Perfect Piecer (Jinny Beyer) to mark my dots with a Chaco liner pen (Clover). These markers come in all different colors. Marking these dots accurately is crucial for your piecing to be successful.

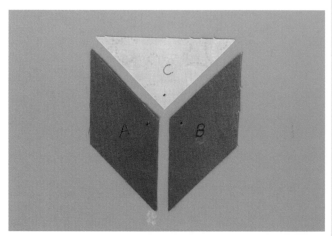

Mark dots precisely.

2. Flip triangle C onto diamond A.

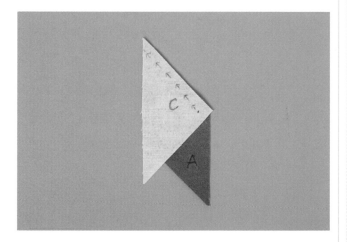

3. Flip the unit. Place a pin through the matching dots on pieces A and C. Start sewing at the pin *at* the dot. Sew 2 stitches forward and then 2 stitches backward. Then continue sewing to the end of the fabric.

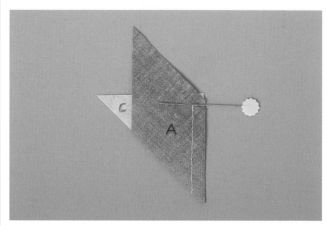

Start sewing right at dot.

 *tip*

TACKING Y-SEAMS

When starting to sew at the dot, it is better to put the needle in front of the pin. This will keep the intersection of the Y nice and flat. The seams need to be tacked at the dots. I like to sew 2 stitches forward and then 2 stitches backward before sewing forward along the seam. Another option is to set the zigzag stitch length to satin stitch and the width to 0. Now the straight stitch is for sewing and the zigzag stitch is programmed into your machine for tacking. Some people like to sew toward the dot, keeping the bias on the underside against the feed dogs. I recommend that you start to sew at the center of the Y and continue to the edge of the fabric piece. The reason I like to start at the dot is that I can put the needle down at the exact starting point, which keeps me from taking an extra stitch at the dot. Try it both ways, and see which way you like best.

4. Open the pieces, and press the seam toward diamond A.

5. Flip diamond B onto triangle C.

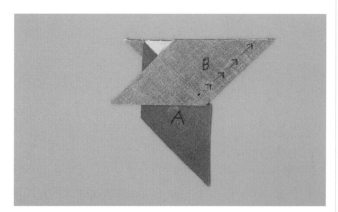

6. Flip the unit. Place a pin through the matching dots. Make sure all the seams are out of the way, so you will be sewing through only 2 layers of fabric. Start sewing at the dot. Sew 2 stitches forward and then 2 stitches backward. Then continue sewing to the end of the fabric.

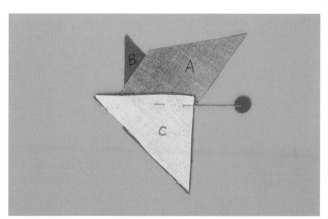

Start sewing right at dot.

7. Open the pieces, and press the seam toward diamond B.

8. Now you are ready to sew the leg of the Y-seam. Fold the unit in half, with the right sides of A and B together. Make sure all the seams are out of the way. Start at the dot, and sew 2 stitches forward and then 2 stitches backward. Continue sewing to the end of the fabric.

Secure stitches at dot.

9. Open the piece, and press the seam clockwise.

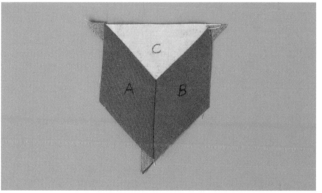

Press seam clockwise.

BLOCKING THE DIAMONDS

Since all diamonds have at least some bias edges, unless you take certain precautions the diamonds will stretch as you piece them together, resulting in lopsided diamonds. To control this problem, you will want to block each large diamond before sewing the Lone Star layout together.

1. Draw the outside diamond at the unfinished size on the nonshiny side of a piece of freezer paper. Then draw an inside line ¼″ from all sides.

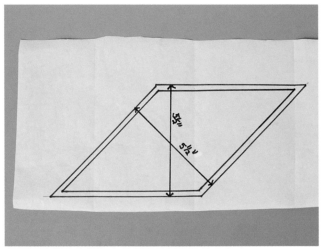

Draw diamond with inside lines.

2. Place the freezer paper on your ironing board with the shiny side down, and iron it to the board.

3. Lay the pieced diamond on top of the freezer-paper drawing, and pin each seamline to the seamline on the drawing.

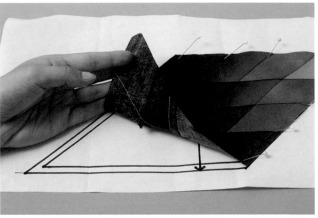

Pin seamline to seamline.

4. Pin around all the seam edges, and lightly mist with water or spray starch. Press the diamonds.

ASSEMBLING THE STAR

You will assemble the star in four quarter-units; each quarter-unit is made up of two large diamonds, a background side triangle, and a corner square.

1. Lay out the diamond and background pieces.

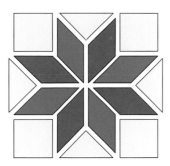

2. Sew together 2 diamonds and the triangle in the seam order shown, adding the corner square with seam 4. This makes a quarter-unit. Check to make sure the diamond points come together. The points must be perfectly aligned to ensure that the center will lie flat. Repeat to make the other 3 quarter-units. Press seams 1 and 2 toward the diamonds. Press seam 3 clockwise. Press seam 4 toward the diamond.

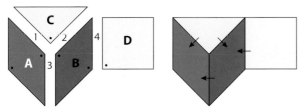

Sew seams in numerical order.

3. Sew 2 units together to make a half-star. Repeat to make the other half-star. Press seam 5 toward the diamond. Press seam 6 clockwise.

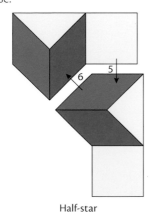

Half-star

4. Sew the 2 half-stars together. I sew the 2 side seams first and finish with the middle seam, always starting at the center of the Y. Be careful to match the diamond points. Press seams 7 and 8 toward the diamonds. See the next step for pressing seam 9.

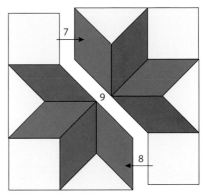

Complete star

5. Before pressing the final seam, remove the vertical stitches in the seam allowances on both sides of each half. Then press the seam allowances in opposite directions. This allows all the Y-seams to be pressed clockwise. Where the 8 diamond points meet in the very center, press the seams open so the seam allowances make a tiny pinwheel.

Getting that center to lie flat

MITERED BORDERS

A border with mitered corners really has a Y-seam at each corner. Here, the quilt is at the 90° angle, and the border pieces are the 135° angles. A quilt can have one mitered border or several mitered borders. If you are making a quilt that has more than one border, sew the pieces for the first border together end to end, making one long piece. Repeat for the second and third borders. Sew the three strips together along their lengths to make one wide border. This wider border section is treated as a single border piece when you add it as a mitered border.

Measuring and cutting

1. To determine the top and bottom border piece lengths, take the average of 3 measurements—one measurement across the quilt top, another across the middle, and the third across the bottom. To this average measurement, add 2 border widths plus 2". This is the border strip length for the top and bottom borders. Cut 2 strips to this measurement. Place pins at the center of each border length, and mark the width of the quilt with pins, measuring from the center pin on the border strips. Each border must measure the same.

2. To determine the side border piece lengths, repeat Step 1, measuring through the vertical center and sides and adding the additional measurements. Cut 2 strips to this measurement. Place pins at the center of each border length, and mark the length of the quilt with pins, measuring from the center pin on the border strips.

3. Pin-mark the center of each side of the quilt. Pin the border strips to the quilt, matching the centers and quilt corners to the pins. Pin as often as needed to work in any fullness.

Sewing the borders

1. Sew each border strip to the quilt, beginning and ending the seam ¼" from the quilt top corners. Backstitch 2 stitches at the start and end of each sewing line.

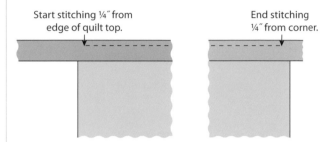

Start stitching ¼" from edge of quilt top.

End stitching ¼" from corner.

2. Fold the quilt corner with right sides together. Press the seams toward the quilt. (They can be pressed toward the border later.) Place a ruler on top of the folded corner. Mark a 45° sewing line, starting where the stitching stopped when the borders were sewn on. If the border is pieced, pin at each border intersection. Sew along this line.

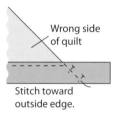

Wrong side of quilt

Stitch toward outside edge.

3. Look at the quilt from the right side to make sure it has a 90° angle. Trim the seams to ¼", and press the seams open.

Front view

STAR QUILTS: SIMPLE TO COMPLEX

Blazing Star, 48″ × 48″, made and machine quilted by Signe Burgen

In this section, you'll find instructions for making nine dazzling wall-size quilts that progress from simple to complex and that will help you build your skills while creating lasting treasures. There's something here for every quilter—from the simple, fussy-cut Gradient Star (page 26) to the twinkling Garland Delight (page 65).

GRADIENT STAR

Made and machine quilted by Barbara Cline

Finished quilt size: 48" × 48"

Diamond layout pattern: 2 × 2

For this quilt, which is the simplest star in this book, you will create your own templates for fussy cutting the diamonds. This quilt gives you plenty of opportunity to perfect those Y-seams. The star's twinkling quality is a result of fussy cutting the individual diamonds from a fabric with a graded-color "stripe" and then arranging them in a particular pattern.

Materials

Yardage is based on 42"-wide fabric.

- **Blue/green/yellow stripe:** 3⅓ yards* (with a 16"–40" repeat from selvage to selvage) for star

- **Background:** 1⅝ yards

- **Binding:** ½ yard

- **Backing:** 3⅛ yards

- **Batting:** 56" × 56"

- **Template plastic**

From this fabric, you must be able to cut out 2 sets of diamonds that are different in value, so they don't blend together in the diamond layout. The repeat in the fabric used here is 21" from selvage to selvage.

Cutting

Background:

- Cut 1 square 21¼" × 21¼"; cut twice diagonally for a total of 4 triangles.

- Cut 2 strips 14½" × WOF*; subcut into 4 squares 14½" × 14½".

Binding:

- Cut 6 strips 2¼" × WOF*.

Blue/green/yellow stripe:

- Cutting instructions for the star diamonds are given in the project steps.

WOF = width of fabric

Making the Template

1. On template plastic, draw 2 parallel lines 17" long and 5½" apart.

2. Draw a line at a 45° angle.

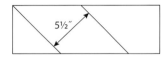

3. Draw a parallel line 5½" from the first line.

4. Mark the template with a grainline (page 16), with arrows toward the 45° angles, and cut out the template.

Making the Large Diamonds

1. To fussy cut (page 16) the diamonds, locate the areas on the striped fabric where your chosen color gradations appear. What creates the twinkling design is the direction in which you turn the diamond tips. As you can see in the photo (page 26), the center diamonds are the green-yellow gradation B diamonds, but they are alternately flipped. These same diamonds appear in the tips of the star; but there the yellow tips all point inward. The illustration below shows how the diamonds were placed for the quilt photo. Make sure you have enough area to cut 16 diamonds of each gradation. Place the template on the striped fabric, and cut out 16 diamond A's and 16 diamond B's.

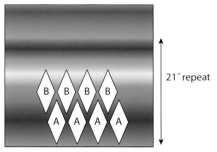

Cut 16 A diamonds and 16 B diamonds.

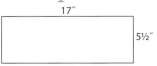

2. Select 2 diamond A's and 2 diamond B's, and place them with the colors as shown to make a large diamond unit C. Be careful on the color placement. Sew A to B as a row, and sew B to A as shown. Press the seams toward the A diamonds. Complete 4 units.

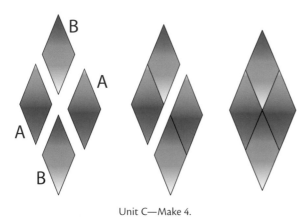

Unit C—Make 4.

3. Select 2 diamond A's and 2 diamond B's, and place them with the colors as shown to make a large diamond unit D. Sew together the diamonds as shown. Press the seams toward the A diamonds. Complete 4 units.

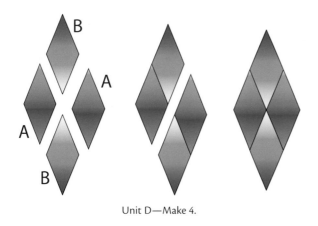

Unit D—Make 4.

4. Refer to Blocking (page 22) to draw the pressing pattern for the large diamond, and then block each large diamond. The outside dimensions for the freezer-paper pattern are 10½″ × 10½″.

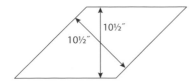

Assembling the Quilt

1. Refer to the photo (page 26) to lay out the large diamond units C and D. Make sure the color tips are in the right positions. Then add the side triangles and the corner squares to the layout.

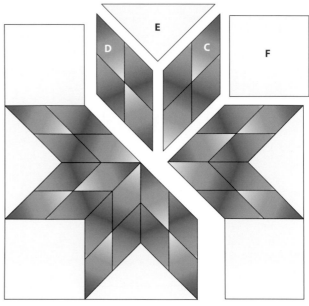

Quilt layout

2. Refer to Y-seams (page 19) to sew the large diamond units C and D to triangle E.

3. Refer to Assembling the Star (page 23) to sew the units from Step 2 to the F squares, and then join the quarters together.

4. Use your favorite methods to layer, quilt, and bind the quilt with the 2¼″ strips. Refer to the photographs for quilting ideas.

Details of quilting

LIFE LESSONS: DO THE JOB RIGHT

As a young Mennonite girl, I always wore home-sewn garments. When I was in the fifth grade, I wanted to make a dress. My mother guided me as I cut out, marked, pinned, and sewed. When the time came for me to sew in the sleeves, I pinned, sewed, turned the sleeves right side out … and I discovered pleats instead of gathers. At this point, I was ready to be done and thought the pleats could just stay. Mother had different ideas. She patiently coached me, teaching me how to use a seam ripper and instructing me on how to place my pins closer together. I tried again, and this time the job was done right. Not only was I pleased with the finished dress, but the satisfaction of knowing the job was done right encouraged me to pursue higher levels of perfection.

LESSON:

Satisfaction can be gained from a job done right.

Made and machine quilted by Barbara Cline

Finished quilt size: 48" × 48"

Diamond layout pattern: 3 × 3

This quilt features three stars-within-stars and uses a somewhat different diamond shape than the one used in *Gradient Star* (page 26). The parallelograms in *Triple Star Splendor* have two 45° angles and two 135° angles, just like the diamonds we have been working with. What makes this diamond different is that instead of all four sides being equal lengths, two sides of the parallelogram are longer than the other two sides, making it look like a *long diamond* (page 17). In this project, you will cut these shapes from strips just as you would cut the basic type of diamonds. For basic instructions on creating strip sets and cutting diamonds from strips and strip sets, see page 18.

Materials

Yardage is based on 42"-wide fabric.

- **Red print:** ¾ yard for first and third stars

- **Red solid:** ⅓ yard for second border

- **Black:** 2⅞ yards for background, first and third borders, second star, and binding

- **Backing:** 3⅛ yards

- **Batting:** 56" × 56"

Cutting

Red print:

- Cut 7 strips 3" × WOF*.

Red solid:

- Cut 6 strips 1½" × WOF*.

Black:

- Cut 1 square 16¼" × 16¼"; cut twice diagonally for a total of 4 triangles, and label each as B.

- Cut 2 strips 11" × WOF*; cut into 4 squares 11" × 11", and label each as C.

- Cut 1 strip 5½" × WOF*.

- Cut 1 strip 3" × WOF*.

- Cut 12 strips 3" × WOF*.

- Cut 6 strips 2¼" × WOF*.

WOF = width of fabric

Making the Large Diamonds

To create the large diamond units, you will cut diamonds from 2 different strip sets and one strip.

STRIP SET 1

1. Following the instructions for strip sets (page 18), sew a red print 3" strip to each side of a black 3" strip as shown, offsetting by the strip width. Press the seams toward the black.

2. Trim off the stairsteps to make a 45° angle. Subcut 8 sections 3" wide as shown.

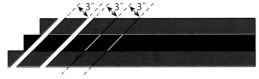

Cut 8 sections.

STRIP SET 2

1. Following the instructions for strip sets (page 18), sew a red print 3" strip to a black 5½" strip as shown. Press the seam toward the black.

2. Trim off the stairsteps to make a 45° angle. Subcut 8 sections 3″ wide as shown.

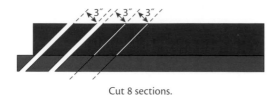

Cut 8 sections.

STRIP 3

From the remaining red print 3″ strips, cut 8 long diamonds 8″ wide. Make sure to cut the angle to the left as shown.

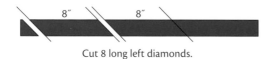

Cut 8 long left diamonds.

Assembling the Large Diamonds

1. Arrange a section from strip set 1, strip set 2, and strip 3 together in sequence as shown. Sew together to make one large diamond (unit A). Press as indicated. Repeat to make a total of 8 large diamonds.

Unit A—Make 8.

2. Refer to Blocking (page 22) to draw the pressing pattern for the large diamond, and then block each large diamond. The outside dimensions for the freezer-paper pattern are 8″ × 8″.

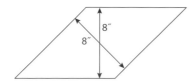

Assembling the Quilt

1. Refer to the quilt photo (page 30) and quilt layout to arrange the large diamond units with the B triangles and the C squares for the quilt center. Refer to Y-seams (page 19) to sew together the large diamonds and background pieces in the order shown for each quarter. Then refer to Assembling the Star (page 23) to join the quarters to complete the quilt center.

Quilt layout

2. Refer to Mitered Borders (page 24) to add the borders. Use the black 3″ strips and the solid red 1½″ strips. The red border is placed between 2 black borders. Sew the strips together, and add them to the quilt as a single unit on each side of the quilt.

3. Use your favorite methods to layer, quilt, and bind the quilt with the 2¼″ strips. A suggested quilting design is shown.

Detail of quilting

LIFE LESSONS: LEARNING DISCIPLINE

When I was young, my father often worked away from home, leaving the family in the care of my capable mother. An important part of each day was spent sharing a Bible story and singing several hymns together. On one such occasion, I was interrupting our devotions by pestering my older sisters. Mother gave me a stern warning, which fell on deaf ears. As soon as I realized I had crossed the line, I begged for mercy to escape the punishment. Mother was firm and came through with her promised discipline.

I learned that I was never too old to be in need of discipline. My mother's loving, firm hand taught me how to order my life. This discipline applied to other areas in my life, such as sewing projects. One rule Mother had was that we could never start a second sewing project until we had finished the first. To this day, I may have several projects going at one time, but I will work on them all. If the project isn't turning out like I thought it would and the temptation is to stick it back in the closet forever, I put it in my basket and wait until a new idea hits. I know I will get it out and finish the project.

LESSON: *Discipline is needed for a well-ordered life.*

Made and machine quilted by Barbara Cline

Finished quilt size: 48" × 48"

Diamond layout pattern: 5 × 5

To create a border behind the star, we need to piece the four background squares and the four background triangles of the diamond layout. In *Star Reflections*, a yellow border is set just behind the star so that the star appears to extend beyond the quilt center. This is achieved with piecing in the background. Be creative and change the squares and triangles of the backgrounds to come up with a unique design for your background.

Materials

Yardage is based on 42"-wide fabric.

- **Red A:** ⅛ yard for star tips (darkest red)
- **Red B:** ¼ yard for stars
- **Red C:** ⅛ yard for stars
- **Red D:** ⅛ yard for stars
- **Red E:** ¼ yard for stars
- **Red F:** ⅓ yard for stars
- **Red G:** ⅓ yard for stars
- **Red H:** ¼ yard for stars
- **Brown:** 2⅜ yards for background, stars, and second border
- **Yellow print:** ½ yard for first border
- **Yellow solid:** ⅓ yard for third border
- **Binding:** ½ yard
- **Backing:** 3⅛ yards
- **Batting:** 56" × 56"

Cutting

Red A, C, and D:

- Cut 1 strip 2¼" × WOF*.

Red B, E, and H:

- Cut 2 strips 2¼" × WOF*.

Red F and G:

- Cut 3 strips 2¼" × WOF*.

Brown:

- Cut 10 strips 2¼" × WOF*; label this fabric I.
- Cut 2 strips 11" × WOF*; subcut 4 squares 11" × 11".
- Cut 1 square 15¼" × 15¼"; cut twice diagonally for a total of 4 triangles.
- Cut 6 strips 3" × WOF*.

Yellow print:

- Cut 6 strips 2¼" × WOF*; subcut 4 rectangles 2¼" × 20" and 8 rectangles 2¼" × 15".

Yellow solid:

- Cut 6 strips 1" × WOF*.

Binding:

- Cut 6 strips 2¼" × WOF*.

WOF = width of fabric

Making the Star

MAKING THE LARGE DIAMONDS

1. Refer to Creating a Strip Set (page 18) to make strip sets 1, 2, 3, 4, and 5 as shown (below and page 36). Using a 2¼" offset from row to row will maximize the number of strips you can cut from each strip set. When the strips are sewn together, the width of each set must measure 9¼". Press the seams as indicated by the arrows. Then cut 8 diamond strips 2¼" wide from each strip set as shown. Be sure to label the diamond strips from each strip set.

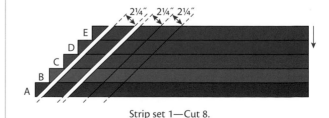

Strip set 1—Cut 8.

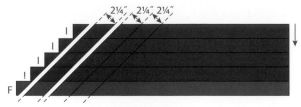

Strip set 2—Cut 8.

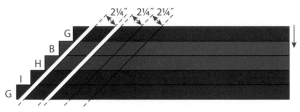

Strip set 3—Cut 8.

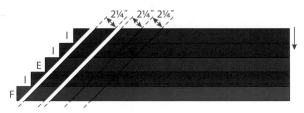

Strip set 4—Cut 8.

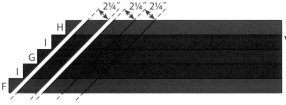

Strip set 5—Cut 8.

2. Arrange a diamond strip from each strip set to make 4 large diamonds as shown. Sew the strips together, and press the seams toward strip set 1. Mark these as unit A.

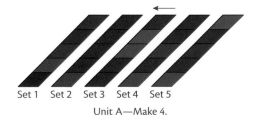

Set 1 Set 2 Set 3 Set 4 Set 5

Unit A—Make 4.

3. Repeat Step 2, *except on strip set 5, rotate the strip end for end.* Make 4 large diamonds as shown. Mark these as unit B.

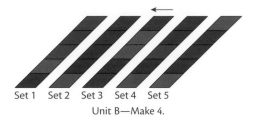

Set 1 Set 2 Set 3 Set 4 Set 5

Unit B—Make 4.

4. Refer to Blocking (page 22) to press the diamonds into the proper size and shape. The outside dimensions for the freezer-paper diamond pattern are 9¼" × 9¼". Block each large diamond.

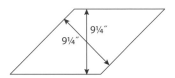

9¼"

9¼"

SEWING THE BACKGROUND TRIANGLES TO THE FIRST BORDER

The first border is added to the background squares and triangles before the quilt top is assembled.

1. With right sides together, center the yellow 2¼" × 20" rectangle on top of the brown background triangle. The ends of the yellow piece will extend beyond the triangle. Sew the section together.

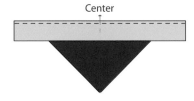

Center

2. Press the seam toward the triangle. Use a ruler and rotary cutter to trim off the extended ends so they are even with the edges of the triangle. Repeat these steps to make 4, and mark as unit C.

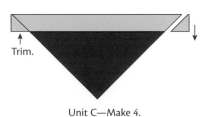

Trim.

Unit C—Make 4.

SEWING THE BACKGROUND SQUARES TO THE FIRST BORDER

Refer to Mitered Borders (page 24) to add 2 yellow 2¼" × 15" strips to 2 adjacent sides of a brown 11" square. Miter 1 corner as shown. Trim the extended ends even with the edges of the square. Repeat for each of the quilt corner squares.

Unit D—Make 4.

Assembling the Quilt

1. Refer to the quilt layout to arrange the alternating large diamonds with the corner squares and side triangles for the quilt center. Refer to Y-seams (page 19) to sew the large diamonds and background pieces together for each quarter. Then refer to Assembling the Star (page 23) to join the quarters and complete the quilt center.

Quilt layout

2. Refer to Mitered Borders (page 24). Use the yellow 1" strips and the brown 3" strips to make a pieced, mitered border, with the yellow as the final border to the outside of the quilt top. Refer to the quilt photo (page 34) to check the color placement for the borders.

3. Use your favorite methods to layer, quilt, and bind the quilt with the 2¼" strips. A suggested quilting design is shown below.

Detail of quilting

Made and machine quilted by Barbara Cline

Finished quilt size: 48" × 48"

Diamond layout pattern: 1 × 1

In this 1 × 1 diamond layout, smaller blue and lavender stars appear to overlap the points of the large dark-colored star. To create this effect, diamond units are broken down into diamonds and triangles, and the diamonds are broken down a step further into strip piecing. In the background, the breakdown process continues with diamonds and triangles.

Choosing fabrics for this quilt can be tricky. You need fabrics in two colorways, plus a large star fabric and a background fabric. Each colorway has a light, medium, and dark value.

Keep in mind that the dark value used in the small stars should contrast with the large star, and that the light value in the small stars should contrast with the background fabric. For more information on value, see Choosing Color (page 9).

Materials

All yardage is based on 42″-wide fabric.

- **Light purple:** ¼ yard for strips in star
- **Medium purple:** ¼ yard for strips in star
- **Dark purple:** ¼ yard for strips in star
- **Light blue:** ¼ yard for strips in star
- **Medium blue:** ¼ yard for strips in star
- **Dark blue:** ¼ yard for strips in star
- **Black:** ⅝ yard for large star
- **Background:** 1⅜ yards
- **Dark print:** 1 yard for outer border
- **Binding:** ½ yard
- **Backing:** 3⅛ yards
- **Batting:** 56″ × 56″

Cutting

Light purple:

- Cut 3 strips 1½″ × WOF*.
- Cut 1 strip 2½″ × WOF*; subcut 2 squares 2½″ × 2½″, and cut diagonally once for a total of 4 triangles.

Medium purple:

- Cut 3 strips 1½″ × WOF*.

Dark purple:

- Cut 3 strips 1½″ × WOF*.

Light blue:

- Cut 3 strips 1½″ × WOF*.

Medium blue:

- Cut 3 strips 1½″ WOF*.
- Cut 1 strip 2½″ × WOF*; subcut 2 squares 2½″ × 2½″, and cut diagonally once for a total of 4 triangles.

Dark blue:

- Cut 3 strips 1½″ × WOF*.

Black:

- Cut 2 strips 7¼″ × WOF*; subcut 8 squares 7¼″ × 7¼″, and cut diagonally twice for a total of 32 triangles.

Background:

- Cut 1 strip 11⅛″ × WOF*; subcut 2 squares 11⅛″ × 11⅛″, and cut diagonally once for a total of 4 triangles.
- Cut 2 strips 7¼″ × WOF*; subcut 6 squares 7¼″ × 7¼″, and cut diagonally twice for a total of 24 triangles.
- Cut 6 strips 3″ × WOF*.

Dark print:

- Cut 6 strips 4½″ WOF*.

Binding:

- Cut 6 strips 2¼″ × WOF*.

*WOF = width of fabric

Make 3 strip sets. Cut 20 sections.

Make 3 strip sets. Cut 20 sections.

MAKING THE LARGE DIAMONDS

1. Make a large blue diamond unit using 4 black triangles and 3 small blue diamond units as shown. Refer to Y-seams (page 19), and complete the Y-seams before adding the black diamond tip triangles. Press the last triangles toward the small diamond unit. Repeat to make a total of 4 large blue diamonds.

Make 4.

2. Repeat Step 1 to make 4 large purple diamonds, using 4 black triangles and 3 small purple diamond units.

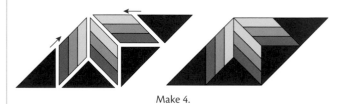

Make 4.

3. Cut a 2" × 2" square of paper, and then cut it in half diagonally. Use this as a pattern for trimming the tips from the large diamond units. Position the paper triangle on a large diamond tip. Cut the tip. Repeat on each large diamond. Make sure all 8 diamond tips are trimmed on the same end.

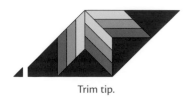

Trim tip.

Making the Star

MAKING THE SMALL DIAMOND UNITS

These strip sets are for left diamond cuts (page 17). Following the instructions for strip sets (page 17), sew light, medium, and dark strips together in sequence, offsetting each strip 1½" as shown. Keep the darkest fabric on the bottom and the lightest fabric on top. Sew 3 sets of each colorway. Press the seams as shown. Trim off the stairsteps to make a 45° cut as shown. Cut 20 diamond units 3½" wide from each colorway for a total of 20 purple and 20 blue small diamond units.

4. Sew a triangle cut from the 2½" squares to each large diamond as shown. The large purple diamond has a small blue triangle added, and the large blue diamond gets a small purple triangle. Press toward the black.

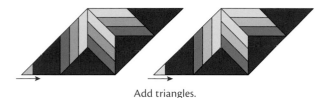

Add triangles.

5. Refer to Blocking (page 22) to press the diamonds into the proper size and shape. The outside dimensions for the freezer-paper pattern are 7¾" × 7¾". Block each large diamond section.

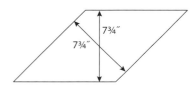

MAKING THE BACKGROUND TRIANGLES AND SQUARES

1. Arrange 3 background triangles cut from the 7¼" squares and 2 small blue diamond units to make the triangle unit as shown. Sew the Y-seams first, and then add the corner triangles. Make 4 blue units. Then make 4 purple triangle units.

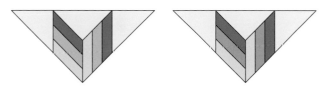

Make 4 of each color.

2. Sew a large background triangle to a purple triangle unit from Step 1, and press. Make 4 corner squares as shown.

Make 4.

Assembling the Quilt

1. Arrange the star center following the quilt layout. Refer to Y-seams (page 19) and Assembling the Star (page 23) to sew the units into quarters, and then join the quarters.

Quilt layout

2. Refer to Mitered Borders (page 24). Use the background 3" strips and the dark print 4½" strips to make a pieced mitered border with the dark print as the outside border.

3. Use your favorite methods to layer, quilt, and bind the quilt with the 2¼" strips. Refer to the quilt detail photos on pages 40 and 42 for quilting design ideas.

LIFE LESSONS: A LESSON IN LEARNING

Math was an easy subject for me in my early elementary school years. I enjoyed good grades and impressive report cards until I encountered those dreadful "greater than" and "less than" symbols in fourth grade. I could understand 6 < 9 and 2 < 5. The concept that confused me was when the larger number was on the left: Was it 6 < 2 or 6 > 2? I remember being disturbed by the red ink marks on my math paper as I struggled to understand this concept. Bewildered and confused, I went to my teacher for help. She patiently explained the concept to me, and a light bulb came on for me when I finally understood.

I learned that day the importance of seeking help when I didn't understand what was being taught. I was also impressed by my gentle teacher, who was willing to keep working with me until I had conquered the problem.

Today when a student in my quilting class has trouble understanding what I am teaching, I enjoy instructing until the lesson is learned.

LESSON: *Ask for help, and keep working until the concept is mastered.*

Made and machine quilted by Barbara Cline

Finished quilt size: 48″ × 48″

Diamond layout pattern: 3 × 3

The techniques used in *Star Ripple* include strip piecing, piecing smaller diamond units, and appliquéing. Here, a ring of pieced and appliquéd diamonds is made in a color pattern that is the reverse of the one used in the diamonds within the star.

Materials

Yardage is based on 42″-wide fabric.

- **Light green:** ⅝ yard
- **Green:** ½ yard
- **Light blue:** ½ yard
- **Dark blue:** ¼ yard
- **Medium blue:** ⅜ yard for second star
- **Background:** 1⅝ yards for background and first border
- **Main bright print:** ⅞ yard for second border
- **Binding:** ½ yard
- **Backing:** 3⅛ yards
- **Batting:** 56″ × 56″
- **HeatnBond Lite:** ½ yard

Cutting

When cutting fabric strips to make diamonds, make sure all the fabric is right side up. All diamond cuts are to the right for right diamonds. Label all the pieces.

Light green:

- Cut A pieces—6 strips 1″ × WOF*; subcut 3″ long right diamonds for a total of 48.
- Cut B pieces—4 strips 1″ × WOF*.
- Cut C pieces—2 strips 2″ × WOF*.

Green:

- Cut D pieces—6 strips 1″ × WOF*; subcut 3″ long right diamonds for a total of 48.
- Cut E pieces—4 strips 1″ × WOF*.

Light blue:

- Cut F pieces—4 strips 1″ × WOF*; subcut 3″ long right diamonds for a total of 32.
- Cut G pieces—4 strips 1″ × WOF*.
- Cut H pieces—2 strips 2″ × WOF*.

Dark blue:

- Cut I pieces—2 strips 2″ × WOF*.

Medium blue:

- Cut J pieces—3 strips 3″ × WOF*; subcut 3″ diamonds for a total of 24.

Background:

- Cut side triangles—1 square 16¼″ × 16¼″; cut twice diagonally for a total of 4 triangles.
- Cut corners—2 strips 11⅛″ × 11⅛″; subcut 4 squares 11⅛″ × 11⅛″.
- Cut first border—6 strips 2½″ × WOF*.

Main bright print:

- Cut second border—6 strips 4⅜″ × WOF*.

Binding:

- Cut 6 strips 2¼″ ×WOF*.

HeatnBond Lite:

- Cut 4 strips 3½″ × WOF*; subcut 3½″ diamonds for a total of 16 pieces.

*WOF = width of fabric

Making the Small Diamond Units

1. Following the instructions for strip sets (page 18), sew 2 B strips and 1 H strip together as shown. Make 2 sets. Trim off the stairsteps to make a 45° angle. Cut 24 diamond strips 2″ wide from the strip set B-H-B.

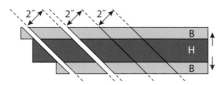

Make 2 strip sets. Cut 24.

2. Sew the A pieces to the sides of a B-H-B diamond strip set as shown. Repeat to make 24.

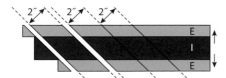

Make 24.

3. Sew 2 E strips and 1 I strip together as shown. Make 2 sets. Trim off the stairsteps to make a 45° angle as shown. Cut 24 diamond strips 2″ wide from the strip set E-I-E.

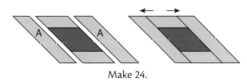

Make 2 strip sets. Cut 24.

4. Sew D pieces to the sides of an E-I-E diamond strip set as shown. Make 24.

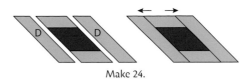

Make 24.

5. Sew 2 G strips and 1 C strip together as shown. Make 2 strip sets. Trim off the stairsteps to make a 45° angle. Cut 16 diamond strips 2″ wide from the strip set G-C-G.

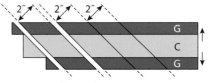

Make 2 strip sets. Cut 16.

6. Sew F pieces to the sides of strip set G-C-G as shown. Make 16.

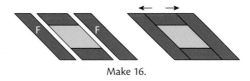

Make 16.

7. Iron the 3½″ × 3½″ piece of HeatnBond Lite to the back of the piece from Step 6. (*Note:* The HeatnBond Lite piece will be larger than the pieced diamond.) Trim ¼″ from each side of the pieced diamond so it measures 2½″ × 2½″. Peel the paper from the back of the diamond, and set these small diamond units aside to be added to the quilt top later.

Making the Large Diamonds

1. To assemble a large diamond, place the light small diamond units with the medium blue J diamonds as shown. Sew the rows together to form the large diamond. Make 4 large diamonds from the light fabrics.

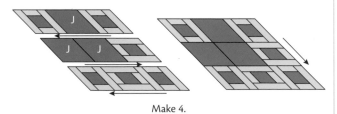

Make 4.

2. Repeat Step 1, using the small diamond units with the dark blue as shown. Make 4 large diamonds.

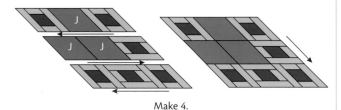

Make 4.

3. Refer to Blocking (page 22) to press the diamonds into the proper size and shape. The outside dimensions for the freezer-paper pattern are 8″ × 8″. Block each large diamond section.

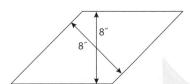

Assembling the Quilt

1. Lay out the large diamonds, alternating them in the center as shown in the layout. Add the corner squares and the side triangles. Refer to Y-seams (page 19), and sew the pieces into quarters. Then join the quarters, referring to Assembling the Star (page 23).

Quilt layout

2. Follow the instructions in Mitered Borders (page 24) to add the outer borders to the quilt, using the background 2½″ strips and the bright print 4⅜″ strips. Join the strips together, and add as a border unit to each side of the quilt.

Appliquéing the Ring of Diamonds

1. Refer to the quilt photo (page 43) for placement of the ring of small diamond units in the star background. Iron the diamonds in place.

2. Attach a ¼" foot to your sewing machine, and set the stitch width to 2mm and the stitch length to 1mm. The ¼" foot will have only a 2mm opening, so the needle will just miss the foot. This will keep the fabric from riding up on the needle and missing stitches. I prefer using the straight-stitch plate because it helps prevent skipped stitches.

3. Appliqué the diamonds onto the quilt, tacking at the beginning and end with a small straight stitch.

4. Use your favorite methods to layer, quilt, and bind the quilt with the 2¼" strips. The quilt detail photo (at right) shows my quilting designs for this quilt.

Quilting suggestion

Star Ripple, 48" × 48", made and machine quilted by Susan Graham

Made by Barbara Cline and machine quilted by Patricia Bird

Finished quilt size: 48" × 48"

Diamond layout pattern: 7 × 7

The diamond layout in the center of *Midnight Star* was created by strip piecing. The background squares were pieced with four 8-pointed stars before the borders were added.

When choosing the fabrics for the diamond layout, use tone-on-tone prints, marbled fabrics, or solids rather than multicolored prints that will distract your eye from the pattern as a whole. It is also important that you choose four distinct values of the four red fabrics in the star points to keep the quilt from getting a big mass of red circling the star.

Small background star

Materials

Yardage is based on 42"-wide fabric.

- **White:** ⅜ yard
- **Dark red:** ⅜ yard for star
- **Medium red:** ½ yard for star
- **Light red:** ⅝ yard for star
- **Lightest red:** ¾ yard for star
- **Light gray:** ⅞ yard
- **Black:** 2¼ yards for background and second border
- **Red:** ⅓ yard for first border

- **Binding:** ½ yard
- **Backing:** 3⅛ yards
- **Batting:** 56" × 56"
- **Template plastic**

Cutting

Label all the pieces. The Midnight Star *template pattern is on page 92.*

White:

- Cut A—2 strips 1¾" × WOF*.
- Cut I—2 strips 1¾" × WOF*; subcut 1¾" diamonds for a total of 16.

Dark red star:

- Cut B—4 strips 1¾" × WOF*.

Medium red star:

- Cut C—6 strips 1¾" × WOF*.

Light red star:

- Cut D—8 strips 1¾" × WOF*.

Lightest red star:

- Cut F—10 strips 1¾" × WOF*.

Light gray:

- Cut F—12 strips 1¾" ×WOF*.
- Cut H—2 strips 1¾" × WOF*; subcut 1¾" diamonds for a total of 16.

Black:

- Cut G—7 strips 1¾" × WOF*.
- Cut J—1 strip 2¼" × WOF*; subcut 16 squares 2¼" × 2¼".
- Cut K—1 strip 3¾" × WOF*; subcut 4 squares 3¾" × 3¾", and cut diagonally twice for a total of 16 triangles.
- Cut L—6 strips 3⅝" × WOF*; subcut 16 pieces using the *Midnight Star* template pattern.

Cutting list continued

- Cut side triangles—1 square 18¾″ × 18¾″; subcut diagonally twice for a total of 4 triangles.

- Cut 6 strips 2¾″ × WOF*.

Red border:

- Cut 6 strips 1¼″ × WOF*.

Binding:

- Cut 6 strips 2¼″ × WOF*.

WOF = width of fabric

Making the Large Diamonds

1. Following the instructions for strip sets (page 18), sew the strips together as shown, offsetting the strips by 1¾″. Trim the left edge of the set to make a 45° angle. Cut 16 diamond strips 1¾″ wide from strip sets 1, 2, and 3. Cut 8 diamond strips 1¾″ wide from strip set 4.

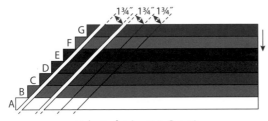

Make 2 of strip set 1. Cut 16.

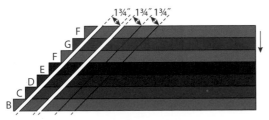

Make 2 of strip set 2. Cut 16.

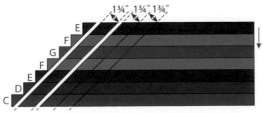

Make 2 of strip set 3. Cut 16.

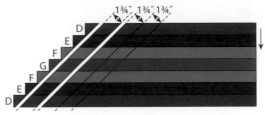

Make 1 of strip set 4. Cut 8.

2. Arrange the diamond strips as shown for the large diamond. Numbers indicate the original strip set numbers. Press. Make 8 large diamonds.

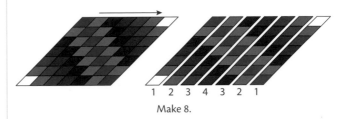

1 2 3 4 3 2 1

Make 8.

3. Refer to Blocking (page 22) to press the diamonds into the proper size and shape. The outside dimensions for the freezer-paper pattern are 9¼″ × 9¼″. Block each large diamond section.

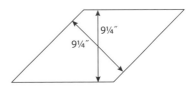

Making the Small Corner Stars

1. Use pieces H, I, J, and K to lay out 4 small stars for the quilt corners, referring to Y-seams (page 19) and Assembling the Star (page 23). Make 4 stars.

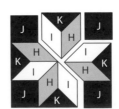

Make 4.

2. Add an L piece to each side of a small star, mitering each corner. Press the seams toward L. Complete 4 blocks.

Make 4.

Assembling the Quilt

1. Lay out *Midnight Star* as shown in the quilt layout. Refer to Assembling the Star (page 23) to sew the top into quarters, and then join the quarters.

Quilt layout

2. To add the borders, refer to Mitered Borders (page 24). Use the red 1¼" strips and the black 2¾" strips to make the border.

3. Use your favorite methods to layer, quilt, and bind the quilt with the 2¼" strips.

LIFE LESSONS: NEVER SAY NEVER

My parents' purchase of a small fabric store became a life-changing event for me. I was eleven when I began measuring fine-printed fabric and stocking shelves with the clothing that catered to the local Mennonite clientele.

My keenness for fabric was honed as the store moved and expanded several times. We began selling sewing machines, and I became a teenage instructor for the Bernina classes. As I droned on about how to maximize this amazing machine and get the fullest benefit from each presser foot, I decided that teaching was *not* for me.

A charming young man entered my life, and my interest in teaching waned as our relationship progressed. After marriage and the birth of our first child, I walked out of the classroom, quite positive I would never return.

Today I am a quilt instructor, and I love what I'm doing. I'm teaching something I'm passionate about. I love to see my students learn new techniques and produce lovely quilts and wallhangings.

Now I never say "never" because I've returned to something I had declared I would never do.

LESSON: *Never say "never," for we may need to eat our words.*

BLAZING STAR

Made and machine quilted by Barbara Cline

Finished quilt size: 48″ × 48″

Diamond layout pattern: 8 × 8

When picking colors for *Blazing Star*, you will need two colorways and eleven different fabrics for the diamonds. You will also need to pick a background color. In *Midnight Star*, we chose tone-on-tone prints, solids, and marbled fabric; the same applies to *Blazing Star*. These fabrics will keep your eye from being distracted from the pattern as a whole.

Notice that this quilt has two different stars, one inside the other. When choosing the fabrics for the two colorways, be sure to choose four or five values in each, starting with dark and graduating to light. You should also choose two contrasting colors for the center stars so that they will jump out from the background.

Once you have chosen all the fabrics, lay them out in the order of the top row of this diamond. This will help you visualize what is going to happen in your star. Notice that fabric B is also the outer tip of the large star. Fabric B needs to contrast with the background fabric. Fabric I should jump out beside fabrics F and G. This all plays a part in creating two stars with depth within the quilt. The quilting on this quilt adds a lot of texture and interest; included are suggestions for quilting.

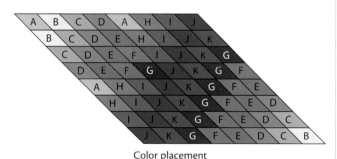

Color placement

Materials

Yardage is based on 42"-wide fabric.

- **Orange (A):** ⅓ yard
- **Yellow/green (B):** ⅓ yard
- **Light green (C):** ⅜ yard
- **Green (D):** ½ yard
- **Dark green (E):** ½ yard
- **Red/green (F):** ½ yard
- **Dark red (G):** ½ yard
- **Orange/red (H):** ⅜ yard
- **Light red (I):** ½ yard
- **Red/orange (J):** ⅝ yard (plus 1 yard if border option 2*)
- **Medium red (K):** ½ yard
- **Background:** 1⅛ yards
- **Binding:** ½ yard
- **Backing:** 3⅛ yards
- **Batting:** 56" × 56"

*If you wish, you can cut border option 1 from scraps of all the fabrics, as shown in the project photo (page 52), or use the red/orange fabric for border option 2.

Cutting

Label all the fabric pieces.

Orange:

■ Cut A—3 strips 1¾″ × WOF*.

Yellow/green:

■ Cut B—3 strips 1¾″ × WOF*.

Light green:

■ Cut C—5 strips 1¾″ × WOF*.

Green:

■ Cut D—7 strips 1¾″ × WOF*.

Dark green:

■ Cut E—7 strips 1¾″ × WOF*.

Red/green:

■ Cut F—7 strips 1¾″ × WOF*.

Dark red:

■ Cut G—7 strips 1¾″ × WOF*.

Orange/red:

■ Cut H—4 strips 1¾″ × WOF*.

Light red:

■ Cut I—6 strips 1¾″ × WOF*.

Red/orange:

■ Cut J—8 strips 1¾″ × WOF*.

Medium red:

■ Cut K—7 strips 1¾″ × WOF*.

Background:

■ Cut 1 square 14⅝″ × 14⅝″; cut twice diagonally.

■ Cut 4 squares 11¼″ × 11¼″.

Binding:

■ Cut 6 strips 2¼″ × WOF*.

Border options:

Border option 1—from scraps:

■ Cut 172 rectangles 1¾″ × 3¾″.

Border option 2—from the red/orange:

■ Cut 4 rectangles 3¾″ × 22″.

■ Cut 8 rectangles 3¾″ × 17″.

**WOF = width of fabric*

Making the Large Diamonds

1. Following the instructions for strip sets (page 18), arrange the strips as shown, offsetting 1¾″. Sew the strips together. Trim off the left edge of each set at a 45° angle. Cut 8 strips 1¾″ wide from each set. Label each diamond strip.

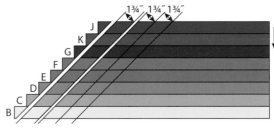

Strip set 1—Cut 8.

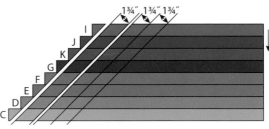

Strip set 2—Cut 8.

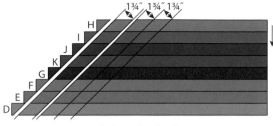

1¾" 1¾" 1¾"

Strip set 3—Cut 8.

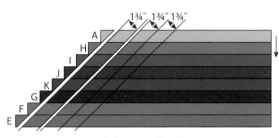

1¾" 1¾" 1¾"

Strip set 4—Cut 8.

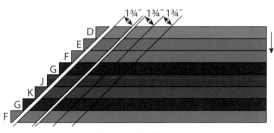

1¾" 1¾" 1¾"

Strip set 5—Cut 8.

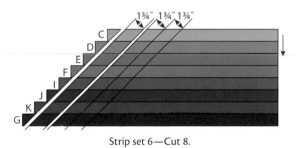

1¾" 1¾" 1¾"

Strip set 6—Cut 8.

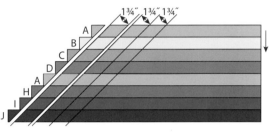

1¾" 1¾" 1¾"

Strip set 7—Cut 8.

1¾" 1¾" 1¾"

Strip set 8—Cut 8.

2. Arrange 8 diamond strips together to form the large diamond. The numbers indicate the origin of the diamond strip. Make 8 large diamonds.

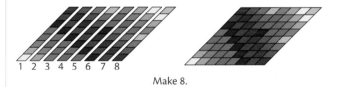

1 2 3 4 5 6 7 8

Make 8.

3. Refer to Blocking (page 22) to press the diamonds into the proper size and shape. The outside dimensions for the freezer-paper pattern are 10½" × 10½". Block each large diamond section.

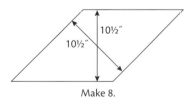

10½"

10½"

Make 8.

Creating the Borders

You can make the borders from assorted fabric scraps or from the red/orange fabric.

1. For border option 1, arrange 13 scrappy rectangles together to make a section 3¾" × 16¾" long as shown. Sew the sections together, and press. Repeat to make a total of 8 sections.

Make 8 sections.

2. Arrange 17 scrappy rectangles together to make a section 3¾" × 21¾". Sew the sections together, and press. Repeat to make a total of 4 sections this size.

3. With right sides together, center a pieced 3¾" × 21¾" strip (for border option 2, use a red 3¾" × 22" rectangle) with a background triangle as shown. The ends of the strip will extend beyond the background piece. Sew, and press the seams toward the border.

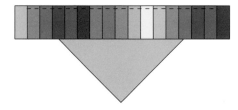

4. Use a ruler and rotary cutter to trim off the extended ends at a 45° angle. Repeat Steps 2 and 3 to complete 4 side triangles.

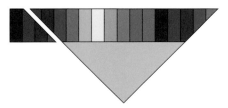
Trim each side.

5. Refer to Mitered Borders (page 24) to add 2 pieced 3¾" × 16¾" border strips (or the red 3¾" × 17" rectangle) to 1 background square, and miter 1 corner as shown. Repeat for each corner square. Trim the extended ends even with the edges of the square.

Make 4.

Assembling the Quilt

1. Refer to the quilt layout to arrange the large diamonds, the side triangles, and the pieced corner squares. Sew each quarter together using Y-seams (page 19). Then refer to Assembling the Star (page 23) to complete the quilt.

Quilt layout

2. Use your favorite methods to layer, quilt, and bind the quilt with the 2¼" strips. Suggested quilting designs are shown in these photos.

Use free-motion quilting to quilt feathers in green diamonds and flames in other diamonds.

On border, stitch in-the-ditch between pieces.

Use walking foot to quilt circles in background behind star.

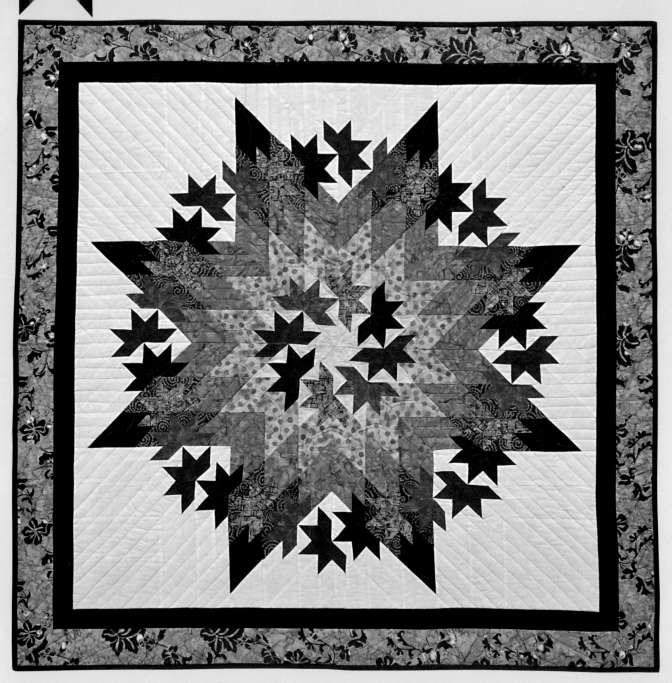

Made and machine quilted by Barbara Cline

Finished quilt size: 48" × 48"

Diamond layout pattern: 3 × 3

This star is more complex than the others in this book because there are many more Y-seams and a greater number of fabrics. When choosing fabrics for the large blue star, choose five shades of fabric, graduating from light to dark. For the small brown stars, choose four shades of fabric, again graduating from light to dark. The key to making the small stars stand out is to have enough contrast between the lightest small star fabric and the lightest large star fabric. In addition, the medium-colored small stars must contrast with the second-darkest blue of the large star.

This quilt is constructed using pieced small diamond units.

Materials

Yardage is based on 42"-wide fabric.

- **Background:** 1¾ yards
- **Dark blue:** 1¼ yards for large star tips, inner border, and binding
- **Medium-dark blue:** ⅓ yard for large star
- **Medium blue:** ⅓ yard for large star
- **Medium-light blue:** ⅓ yard for large star
- **Light blue:** ¼ yard for large star
- **Dark brown:** ¼ yard for small stars
- **Medium brown:** ¼ yard for small stars
- **Medium-light brown:** ¼ yard for small stars
- **Light brown:** ¼ yard for small stars
- **Print:** ⅞ yard for outer border
- **Backing:** 3⅛ yards
- **Batting:** 56" × 56"

Cutting

Label all the pieces as they are cut.

Background:

- Cut A—8 strips 3" × WOF*; subcut 3" diamonds for a total of 64.
- Cut B—3 strips 1½" × WOF*; subcut 2" long right diamonds for a total of 32.
- Cut C—5 strips 2" × WOF*; subcut 3" long right diamonds for a total of 32.
- Cut D—2 strips 3¼" × WOF*; subcut 16 squares 3¼" × 3¼", and cut diagonally twice for a total of 64 triangles.
- Cut Q—1 strip 7½" × WOF*; subcut 4 squares 7½" × 7½".

Dark blue:

- Cut E—1 strip 1½" × WOF*; subcut 2" long right diamonds for a total of 8.
- Cut F—1 strip 2" × WOF*; subcut 3" long right diamonds for a total of 8.
- Cut first border—6 strips 2½" × WOF*.
- Cut binding—6 strips 2¼" × WOF*.

Medium-dark blue:

- Cut G—2 strips 3¼" × WOF*; subcut 16 squares 3¼" × 3¼", and cut diagonally twice for a total of 64 triangles.

Medium blue:

- Cut H—2 strips 1½" × WOF*; subcut 2" long right diamonds for a total of 24.
- Cut I—3 strips 2" × WOF; subcut 3" long right diamonds for a total of 24.

Medium-light blue:

- Cut J—2 strips 1½" × WOF*; subcut 2" long right diamonds for a total of 16.
- Cut K—2 strips 2" × WOF*; subcut 3" long right diamonds for a total of 16.

Cutting list continued

Light blue:

- Cut L—1 strip 3¼″ × WOF*; subcut 8 squares 3¼″ × 3¼″, and cut diagonally twice for a total of 32 triangles.

Dark brown:

- Cut M—3 strips 1½″ × WOF*; subcut 1½″ diamonds for a total of 50.

Medium brown:

- Cut N—3 strips 1½″ × WOF*; subcut 1½″ diamonds for a total of 50.

Medium-light brown:

- Cut O—3 strips 1½″ × WOF*; subcut 1½″ diamonds for a total of 50.

Light brown:

- Cut P—3 strips 1½″ × WOF*; subcut 1½″ diamonds for a total of 50.

Print:

- Cut borders—6 strips 3½″ × WOF*.

WOF = width of fabric

Making the Small Diamond Units

This quilt has two different pieced small diamond units: the small triple-diamond unit and the small single-diamond unit.

SMALL TRIPLE-DIAMOND UNITS

To make the 40 small triple-diamond units, arrange 3 small diamonds and 4 triangles as shown. Refer to Y-seams (page 19). Sew the 2 Y-seams before adding the last 2 triangles. The diagrams for these units give the fabric reference letters. Make the number of units indicated for each colorway, and mark each unit with the proper unit number.

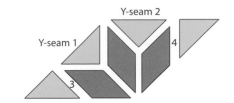

Unit 1—Make 2.

Unit 2—Make 2.

Unit 3—Make 2.

Unit 4—Make 2.

Unit 12—Make 8.

Unit 13—Make 8.

Unit 14—Make 8.

Unit 15—Make 8.

SMALL SINGLE-DIAMOND UNITS

To make the 80 small single-diamond units, arrange a small diamond, a 2″ long right diamond, and a 3″ long right diamond as shown. Sew the 2 upper diamonds together, and then add the bottom long diamond. Press as shown. The diagrams for these units give the fabric reference letters. Make the number of units indicated for each colorway, and mark each unit with the proper unit number.

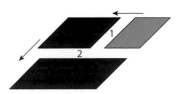

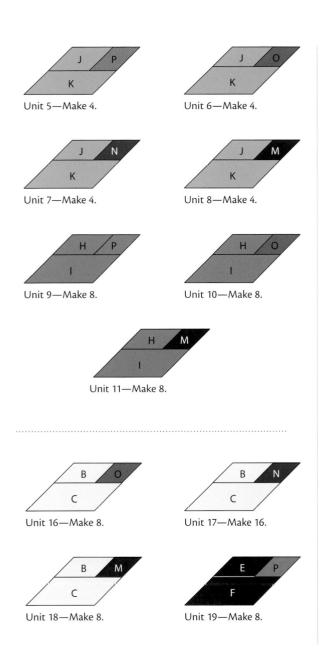

Unit 5—Make 4.

Unit 6—Make 4.

Unit 7—Make 4.

Unit 8—Make 4.

Unit 9—Make 8.

Unit 10—Make 8.

Unit 11—Make 8.

Unit 16—Make 8.

Unit 17—Make 16.

Unit 18—Make 8.

Unit 19—Make 8.

Making the Large Diamonds

1. The star has 4 unique large diamond sections. These are diamond sections rather than complete diamonds, as you will see. Follow the diagram for each diamond section, using the numbered small diamond units as shown and adding individual background A diamonds. Sew each row, and then join the rows together. Press. Make 2 of each large diamond.

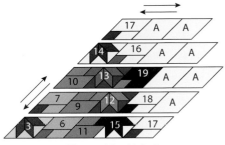

Diamond A—Make 2.

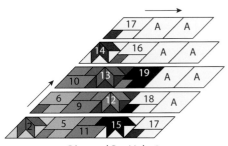

Diamond B—Make 2.

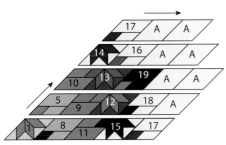

Diamond C—Make 2.

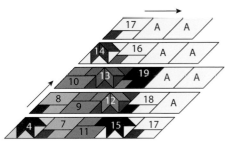

Diamond D—Make 2.

2. Refer to Blocking (page 22) to press the diamonds into the proper size and shape. The outside dimensions for the freezer-paper pattern are 13″ × 13″. Since the diamond sections are not complete diamonds, the pattern will be only partially covered with fabric. Align the outside edges of each diamond section with the pattern, and block.

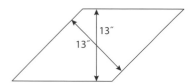

3. After blocking the diamonds, add 2 background A diamonds to each large diamond as shown.

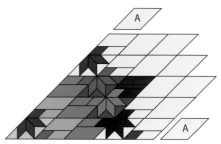

Add 2 background A diamonds.

Assembling the Star

Refer to the quilt star layout to arrange the large diamond sections with the corner background Q squares. Sew the star into quarter sections, using Y-seams (page 19), and then join the quarters together as shown in the star layout. This center section will be trimmed.

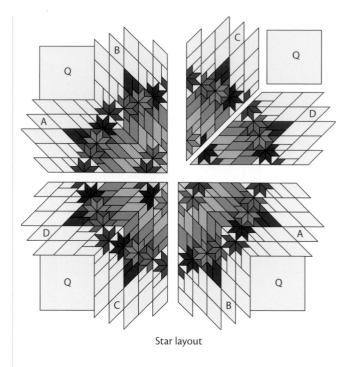

Star layout

Assembling the Quilt Top

1. Refer to the diagram below to mark the star section for a 38½″ square. Use the tips of the star and the center as reference points to help you measure accurately through the quilt center. Trim the section.

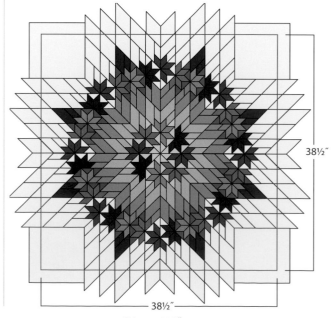

Trim to 38½″ square.

2. Refer to Mitered Borders (page 24) to add the borders to the center. Use the dark blue 2½″ strips and the 3½″ outer border strips.

Quilt layout

3. Use your favorite methods to layer, quilt, and bind the quilt with the 2¼″ strips. A suggested quilting design is shown in the following photos.

Details of quilting

LIFE LESSONS: MY DESIGN FLOOR

My sewing room is an area of heavy traffic. It is located between the living room and the stairway. As I construct a quilt, the pieces rest on the floor for the family to step around or over, depending on the size of the quilt.

One day, I had painstakingly labored over a quilt design for hours. The evening shadows were beginning to fall on the nice arrangement of blocks on my design floor. As a family member traversed the area, he was quick to point out the lack of life in my project. I was crushed as I reflected on the amount of effort I had invested in this fine piece of art. Although I was reluctant to admit it, inside I knew he was right. I listened to his suggestion and rearranged the design. To my amazement, the new look was dazzling.

The extra patter of feet through my sewing room can be frustrating, but I come out the winner when my family's fresh perspective improves my projects.

LESSON: *Always listen to someone else's fresh perspective.*

Made and machine quilted by Barbara Cline

Finished quilt size: 48" × 48"

Diamond layout pattern: 4 × 4

Garland Delight uses the same piecing technique as *Ivy Spangled Banner* (page 58). This quilt has only two different small diamond units to piece. Four stars ripple out from the center, with two rings of stars within the stars. The background corners and side triangles have no additional piecing.

Materials

Yardage is based on 42"-wide fabric.

- **Green:** ⅝ yard for first and third background stars
- **Black:** 1⅛ yards for second and fourth background stars
- **Dark red:** ¼ yard for small stars
- **Medium red:** ¼ yard for small stars
- **Medium-light red:** ¼ yard for small stars
- **Light red:** ¼ yard for small stars
- **Background:** 1½ yards
- **Binding:** ½ yard
- **Backing:** 3⅛ yards
- **Batting:** 56" × 56"

Cutting

Label all the pieces.

Green:

- Cut A—2 strips 3¼" × WOF*; subcut 24 squares 3¼" × 3¼", and cut twice diagonally for a total of 96 triangles.
- Cut B—3 strips 2" × WOF*; subcut 3" long diamonds for a total of 24.
- Cut C—2 strips 1½" × WOF*; subcut 2" long diamonds for a total of 24.

Black:

- Cut D—3 strips 3" × WOF*; subcut 3" diamonds for a total of 24.
- Cut E—2 strips 3¼" × WOF*; subcut 16 squares 3¼" × 3¼", and cut twice diagonally for a total of 64 triangles.
- Cut F—5 strips 2" × WOF*; subcut 3" long diamonds for a total of 40.
- Cut G—3 strips 1½" × WOF*; subcut 2" long diamonds for a total of 40.

Dark red:

- Cut H—3 strips 1½" × WOF*; subcut 1½" diamonds for a total of 42.

Medium red:

- Cut I—3 strips 1½" × WOF*; subcut 1½" diamonds for a total of 42.

Medium-light red:

- Cut J—3 strips 1½" × WOF*; subcut 1½" diamonds for a total of 50.

Light red:

- Cut K—3 strips 1½" × WOF*; subcut 1½" diamonds for a total of 50.

Background:

- Cut 1 square 21¼" × 21¼"; cut twice diagonally for a total of 4 triangles.
- Cut 4 squares 14½" × 14½".

Binding:

- Cut 6 strips 2¼" × WOF*.

*WOF = width of fabric

Making the Small Diamond Units

This quilt has two different pieced small diamond units: the small triple-diamond unit and the small single-diamond unit.

SMALL TRIPLE-DIAMOND UNITS

To make the small triple-diamond units, arrange 3 small diamonds and 4 triangles as shown. Refer to Y-seams (page 19). Sew the Y-seams before adding the last 2 triangles. The diagrams for these units give the fabric reference letters. Make the number of units indicated for each colorway, and mark each unit with the proper unit number.

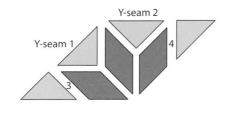

Unit 1—Make 2.

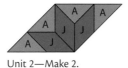

Unit 2—Make 2.

Unit 3—Make 10.

Unit 4—Make 10.

Unit 13—Make 8.

Unit 14—Make 8.

SMALL SINGLE-DIAMOND UNITS

To make the small single-diamond units, arrange a small diamond, a 2"-long right diamond, and a 3"-long right diamond as shown. Sew the 2 upper diamonds together, and then add the bottom long diamond. Press as shown. The diagrams for these units give the fabric reference letters. Make the number of units indicated for each colorway, and mark each unit with the proper unit number.

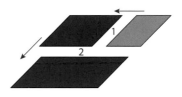

Unit 5—Make 12.

Unit 6—Make 12.

Unit 7—Make 8.

Unit 8—Make 8.

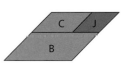

Unit 9—Make 8.

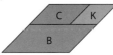

Unit 10—Make 8.

Unit 11—Make 4.

Unit 12—Make 4.

Making the Large Diamonds

1. Arrange all the single-diamond units, the triple-diamond units, and the black 3″ × 3″ diamonds (D) to form the large diamonds. The units are numbered for easy placement. Sew the units into rows, pressing in opposite directions from row to row. Then join the rows, and press. Make 2 of each large diamond. Label each diamond.

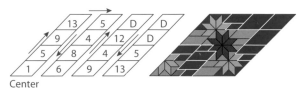

Center

Diamond A—Make 2.

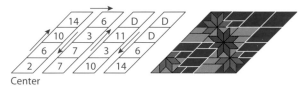

Center

Diamond B—Make 2.

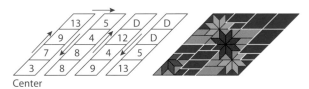

Center

Diamond C—Make 2.

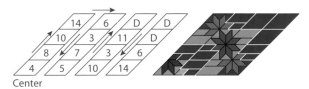

Center

Diamond D—Make 2.

2. Refer to Blocking (page 22) to press the outside diamonds into the proper size and shape. The dimensions for the freezer-paper pattern are 10½″ × 10½″. Block each large diamond.

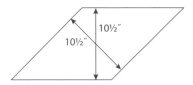

Assembling the Quilt

1. Refer to the quilt layout to arrange the A–D diamonds as shown. Add the corner background squares and the side triangles. Refer to Y-seams (page 19) and Assembling the Star (page 23). Sew each quarter together, and then complete the quilt top.

Quilt layout

2. Use your favorite methods to layer, quilt, and bind the quilt. Suggested quilting designs are shown in these photos.

Quilting on stars

Quilting on background squares

Another variation of *Garland Delight* uses only two different colors of small stars and adds zigzag appliqué in the background squares and triangles.

Floating Ring of Stars, 48" × 48", made and machine quilted by Barbara Cline

LIFE LESSONS: MANY HANDS MAKE LIGHT WORK

Once a year, my family gets together for a sewing retreat. This includes my six sisters, our sister-in-law, and a lot of nieces. It was at one of these retreats that one of us messed up big-time while chain piecing and discovered at the end of the stack that the block had been sewn to the wrong side. Someone suggested that we divide the stack between us and all help rip out. Within a few minutes, the stack was ready to be sewn again.

Now when something like this happens at our sewing retreat, we all know we are there for each other.

I have taken this lesson to the classroom. When a student sews the wrong pieces together, I pick it out for him or her in between teaching. This way the student can continue to sew and learn.

LESSON: *A little help goes a long way.*

CREATE YOUR OWN QUILT

Star Grandeur, 95" × 106", made by Barbara Cline
and hand quilted by Dorothy Messick

*The first three projects in this section show you
how to turn the wall quilts from this book into
full-size and even queen- or king-size quilts.
For these quilts, measurements and fabric
amounts are given for two options: 79½" × 102"
and 96" × 107¼". Simply choose one of the wall
quilts, and match it up with one of the first three
layouts in this section. The blocks in the layouts
are traditional designs, such as Log Cabin and
Hunter's Star.*

*The grand finale of this section uses Midnight
Star as the quilt center and surrounds it with
intricate Delightful Diamond blocks for rich
depth and grandeur—a fitting challenge for
an experienced Lone Star quilter. Chains of
diamonds dance across this quilt.*

*As you choose the star center for these larger
quilts, consider the scale of piecing in each star.
The piecing must be similar in size to that used
in the quilt layout. In this section, experiment
to let your creativity shine through in your own
Lone Star masterpiece.*

STITCHES THAT BIND

Made by Barbara, Parla, Rebecca, and Autumn Cline, and machine quilted by Bonnie Spoon and Barbara Cline

Finished quilt size: 79½″ × 102″

Note: Instructions for a 96″ × 107¼″ quilt are given in parentheses.

The center of this quilt is *Ivy Spangled Banner* (project on page 58) in red, cream, and blue set into a traditional Log Cabin quilt. All the star patterns in this book are finished at 48″ and can be used as quilt centers. When choosing a center for a larger quilt, the scale of piecing should be complementary between the center and the surrounding blocks. Of course, fabric colors in the center, the blocks, and the borders should all coordinate and complement each other.

When selecting fabric for this quilt, I chose a main print that had two colorways. The main fabric has a hint of cream, which I picked up as an accent for the center square of the Log Cabin and for the background fabric behind the large star. The value difference between the floating stars and the large star had to be great enough that the small stars would show. In the large star I added the cream to provide sparkle. This gives a different twist from the *Ivy Spangled Banner* quilt, where the large star is all the same color.

Center star is *Ivy Spangled Banner* (project on page 58), made in same fabrics as Log Cabin blocks.

This Log Cabin pattern has two colorways, each of which includes three distinct values, plus another color for the center square. Choose small prints, solids, or tone-on-tone fabrics. Another option is to choose one colorway and place light-value fabrics on one side of the block and dark-value fabrics on the other side.

In addition, this quilt includes two fabric variations of the Log Cabin block—block 1 has dark red fabric 1 and dark blue fabric 1 on the outside edge, while block 2 has dark red fabric 2 and dark blue fabric 2 on the outside edge.

Materials

This list gives only the yardage for the background blocks and borders. It does not include fabric for the center star. All yardage is based on 42″-wide fabric. The numbers in parentheses are for the 96″ × 107¼″ quilt.

- **Cream:** 1⅛ (1¼) yards for the block centers and first border

- **Light red:** ⅜ (¾) yard

- **Medium red:** ¾ (1⅛) yard

- **Dark red 1:** ⅝ (⅞) yard

- **Dark red 2:** ⅝ (⅞) yard

- **Light blue:** ¾ (1⅛) yard

- **Medium blue:** 1⅛ (1¾) yards

- **Dark blue 1:** ⅞ (1¼) yard

- **Dark blue 2:** ⅞ (1¼) yard

- **Red/blue print:** 1½ (1⅔) yards for the second border

- **Backing:** 7¼ (8⅔) yards

- **Binding:** ¾ (⅞) yard

- **Batting:** 87″ × 110″ (104″ × 115″)

Cutting

Label each piece. The numbers in parentheses are for the 96″ × 107¼″ quilt.

Cream:

- Cut A—3 (5) strips 2¾″ × WOF*; subcut 2¾″ × 2¾″ squares for a total of 36 (60).

- Cut first border—10 (12) strips 2½″ (1¾″) × WOF*.

Light red:

- Cut B—2 (4) strips 2″ × WOF*; subcut 2″ × 2¾″ rectangles for a total of 24 (48).

- Cut C—3 (6) strips 2″ × WOF*; subcut 2″ × 4¼″ rectangles for a total of 24 (48).

Light blue:

- Cut D—4 (7) strips 2″ × WOF*; subcut 2″ × 4¼″ rectangles for a total of 36 (60).

- Cut E—6 (9) strips 2″ × WOF*; subcut 2″ × 5¾″ rectangles for a total of 36 (60).

Medium red:

- Cut F—4 (7) strips 2″ × WOF*; subcut 2″ × 5¾″ rectangles for a total of 24 (48).

- Cut G—5 (10) strips 2″ × WOF*; subcut 2″ × 7¼″ rectangles for a total of 24 (48).

Medium blue:

- Cut H—8 (12) strips 2″ × WOF*; subcut 2″ × 7¼″ rectangles for a total of 36 (60).

- Cut I—9 (15) strips 2″ × WOF*; subcut 2″ × 8¾″ rectangles for a total of 36 (60).

Dark red 1:

- Cut J—3 (6) strips 2″ × WOF*; subcut 2″ × 8¾″ rectangles for a total of 12 (24).

- Cut K—4 (6) strips 2″ × WOF*; subcut 2″ × 10¼″ rectangles for a total of 12 (24).

Dark blue 1:

- Cut L—5 (8) strips 2″ × WOF*; subcut 2″ × 10¼″ rectangles for a total of 18 (30).

- Cut M—6 (10) strips 2″ × WOF*; subcut 2″ × 11¾″ rectangles for a total of 18 (30).

Dark red 2:

- Cut N—3 (6) strips 2″ × WOF*; subcut 2″ × 8¾″ rectangles for a total of 12 (24).

- Cut O—4 (6) strips 2″ × WOF*; subcut 2″ × 10¼″ rectangles for a total of 12 (24).

Dark blue 2:

- Cut P—5 (8) strips 2″ × WOF*; subcut 2″ × 10¼″ rectangles for a total of 18 (30).

- Cut Q—6 (10) strip 2″ × WOF*; subcut 2″ × 11¾″ rectangles for a total of 18 (30).

Red/blue print:

- Cut second border—8 (8) strips 4½″ (2¼″) × length of fabric.

Binding:

- Cut 10 (11) strips 2¼″ × WOF*.

WOF = width of fabric

Making the Blocks and Corner Units

LOG CABIN BLOCKS

Make 12 (24) of block 1; make 12 (24) of block 2. Use the pieces indicated in each block diagram, and sew the pieces together in alphabetical order, creating a red side and a blue side for each block. Press the seams away from the center. Label the blocks.

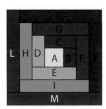 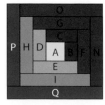

Block 1—Make 12 (24).   Block 2—Make 12 (24).

Log Cabin half-blocks

Make 6 (6) of half-block 1; make 6 (6) of half-block 2. Use the pieces indicated in each half-block, and sew the pieces in alphabetical order. Press the seams away from the center. Label the half-blocks.

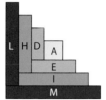 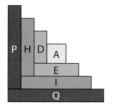

Half-block 1—Make 6 (6).   Half-block 2—Make 6 (6).

Corner units

Arrange blocks 1 and 2 with half-blocks 1 and 2 into the corner units as shown. The upper corner unit and lower corner unit are unique. Sew the triangle units by joining the blocks into rows, and then join the rows. Make 2 of each unit. Press the seams open. Then trim the quarter-units ¼" away from the diagonal block centers as shown.

Make 2 of each. Trim ¼" away from diagonal block centers.

Assembling the Quilt

1. Refer to the quilt layout for the 79½" × 102" quilt to arrange the blocks and half-blocks around the star center you have chosen. If you are making the 96" × 107¼" quilt, you will add a second row to the bottom of the quilt, and you will add a row of blocks to each side of the quilt (see layout on page 86). Make sure that all the blocks are turned the right way. Note that Blocks 1 and 2 alternate throughout the quilt.

Quilt layout, 79½" × 102"

2. Sew the 4 triangle units to the star center. Press the seams toward the star center.

3. Sew the additional blocks into the number of rows indicated for your quilt size. Press the seams open. Sew the additional rows to the quilt.

4. Refer to Mitered Borders (page 24) to add the borders, using the cream 2½" (1¾") strips and the print 4½" (2¼") strips.

5. Use your favorite methods to layer, quilt, and bind the quilt with the 2¼" strips.

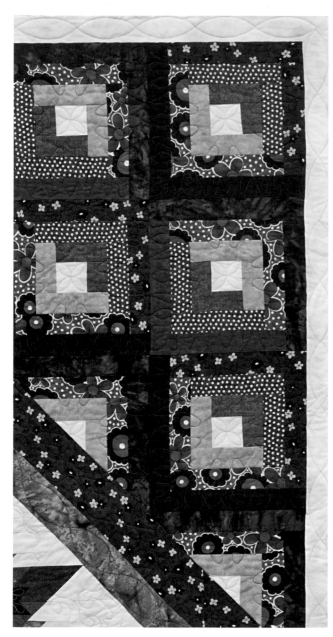 

Details of quilting

STAR STRUCK QUILTS

Made by Barbara Cline and machine quilted by Bonnie Spoon

Finished quilt size: 79½″ × 102″

Note: Instructions for a 96″ × 107¼″ quilt are given in parentheses.

The traditional Hunter's Star pattern is combined here with *Star Reflections* (project on page 34) as the quilt center. Ideas to keep in mind when combining the *Star Reflections* pattern and the Hunter's Star blocks:

■ The last border in *Star Reflections* should not be the same color as the stars in the Hunter's Star blocks.

■ The half-square Hunter's Star blocks need to be a different color than, or a strong value to contrast with, the last border of *Star Reflections*.

■ Consider waiting to select the border fabrics. When piecing this quilt, I chose the borders for the star after the star was pieced. Then I laid the fabrics out beside the finished star and changed and rearranged the fabrics to see which arrangement I liked best.

Center star is *Star Reflections* (project on page 34).

Materials

This list gives only the yardage for the background blocks and borders. It does not include fabric for the center star. Yardage is based on 42"-wide fabric. The numbers in parentheses are for the 96" × 107¼" quilt.

■ **Brown solid:** 1½ (2) yards for stars and first border

■ **Brown print:** ¾ (1⅛) yard for stars

■ **Variety* of yellow print fabrics:** 2¼ (3¼) yards

■ **Variety* of red print fabrics:** 2⅝ (3⅝) yards

■ **Red print:** 1½ (1⅔) yards for the second border

■ **Backing:** 7¼ (8⅔) yards

■ **Binding:** ¾ (⅞) yard

■ **Batting:** 87" × 110" (104" × 115")

■ **Template plastic**

*Choose 8 color values.

Cutting

Label each piece. The numbers in parentheses are for the 96" × 107¼" quilt.

Solid brown:

■ Cut 10 (17) strips 1⅞" × WOF*; subcut 1⅞" diamonds for a total of 120 (216).

■ Cut 10 (12) strips 2½" (1¾") × WOF*.

Brown print:

■ Cut 10 (17) strips 1⅞" × WOF*; subcut 1⅞" diamonds for a total of 120 (216).

Yellow (8 different values):

■ Cut 12 (24) squares 9⅜" × 9⅜"; cut diagonally once for a total of 24 (48) triangles.

■ Cut 15 (24) strips 1⅞" × WOF*; subcut 1⅞" × 8" rectangles for a total of 72 (120).

Red (8 different values):

■ Cut 18 (30) squares 9⅜″ × 9⅜″; cut once diagonally for a total of 36 (60) triangles.

■ Cut 10 (20) strips 1⅞″ × WOF*; subcut 1⅞″ × 8″ rectangles for a total of 48 (96).

Red print:

■ Cut 8 (8) strips 4½″ (2¼″) × length of fabric.

Binding:

■ Cut 10 (11) strips 2¼″ × WOF*.

*WOF = width of fabric

TEMPLATE CUTTING

See the Stellar Inferno *template pattern on page 92.*

1. Use the *Stellar Inferno* template pattern and the yellow 1⅞″ × 8″ pieces to cut the 72 (120) template shapes.

2. Use the *Stellar Inferno* template pattern and the red 1⅞″ × 8″ pieces to cut the 48 (96) template shapes.

Making the Blocks

As you piece the blocks, you will want to mix up the reds, the yellows, and the browns in each block. The solid brown diamonds and the printed brown diamonds always need to be placed in the same position in each block.

1. Sew a solid brown diamond to each left end of all the red and yellow template pieces as shown, and sew a brown print diamond to each right end of all the red and yellow template pieces as shown. Press the seams away from the center. Make 48 (96) red units. Make 72 (120) yellow units.

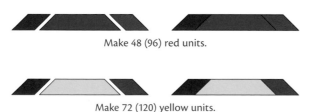

Make 48 (96) red units.

Make 72 (120) yellow units.

2. Sew 2 red units to 1 yellow triangle, referring to Y-seams (page 19). Make 24 (48) yellow half-blocks.

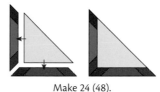

Make 24 (48).

3. Sew 2 yellow units to 1 red triangle, referring to Y-seams (page 19). Make 36 (60) red half-blocks.

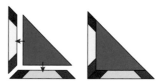

Make 36 (60).

4. Make 24 (48) complete blocks using yellow and red half-blocks as shown.

Make 24 (48).

5. Make 4 (4) triangle units by sewing the blocks into rows and the rows into triangle units. Press the seams open.

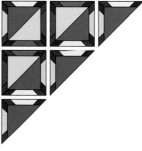

Make 4 (4).

Assembling the Quilt

1. Refer to the quilt layout for the 79½″ × 102″ quilt to arrange the blocks and half-blocks around the star center you have chosen. If you are making the 96″ × 107¼″ quilt, you will add a second row to the bottom of the quilt, and you will add a row of blocks to each side of the quilt (see layout on page 86). Make sure that all the blocks are turned the right way.

2. Sew the 4 triangle units to the star center. Press the seams toward the star.

3. Sew the additional blocks into the number of rows indicated for your quilt size. Press the seams open. Sew the additional rows to the quilt.

4. Refer to Mitered Borders (page 24). Use the solid brown 2½″ (1¾″) strips and the red print 4½″ (2¼″) strips for the borders.

5. Use your favorite methods to layer, quilt, and bind the quilt with the 2¼″ strips. A variety of quilting designs were used in this quilt.

Quilt layout, 79½″ × 102″

Details of quilting

Details of quilting

LOG CABIN AMONG THE STARS

Made by Barbara Cline and machine quilted by Bonnie Spoon

Finished quilt size: 96″ × 107¼″

Note: Instructions for a 79½″ × 102″ quilt are given in parentheses.

I wanted to have two accent colors in this quilt. I chose cream as my first accent color for the stars in the blocks and for the background of the center star. My second accent color was black, which is in the center star, the blocks, and the first border. For the outside border I chose a print with black plus two other colors: green and red. From there I chose five shades of green in different values and five shades of red in different values and used these in the Log Cabin blocks and in the center star.

Center is *Garland Delight* (project on page 65).

Materials

This list gives only the yardage for the background blocks and borders. It does not include fabric for the center star. All yardage is based on 42″-wide fabric. The numbers in parentheses are for the 79½″ × 102″ quilt.

- **Black:** 1 (1) yard for center square and first border

- **Main black print with red and green:** 1⅔ (1½) yards for second border

- **Cream:** 1⅝ (1) yards

- **Light green:** ½ (⅓) yard

- **Medium-light green:** ⅞ (½) yard

- **Medium green:** 1⅛ (¾) yards

- **Medium-dark green:** 1⅛ (⅞) yards

- **Dark green:** 1⅛ (⅞) yards

- **Light red:** ⅞ (½) yard

- **Medium-light red:** 1⅛ (⅞) yards

- **Medium red:** 1½ (1) yards

- **Medium-dark red:** 1⅛ (⅞) yards

- **Dark red:** 1⅛ (⅞) yards

- **Backing:** 8⅔ (7¼) yards

- **Binding:** ⅞ (¾) yard

- **Batting:** 104″ × 115″ (87″ × 110″)

- **Template plastic**

3. Trim the blocks ¼" to the left of center as shown.

Trim ¼" from
left of center.

Assembling the Quilt Top

1. Refer to the quilt layout for the 96" × 107¼" quilt to arrange the blocks and half-blocks around the star center you have chosen. If you are making the 79½" × 102" quilt, you will not add the second row to the bottom of the quilt, and you will not add the side rows of blocks. Arrange the blocks around the center star, alternating a dark-edged block with a medium-dark–edged block. Make sure there are no two fabrics alike beside each other and that all the blocks are turned the right way. Check the color placement throughout the quilt.

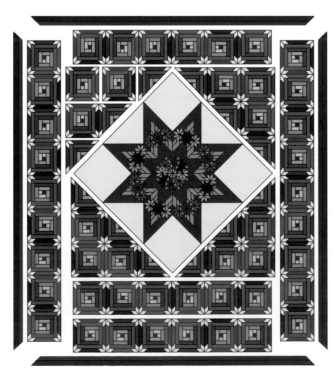

Quilt layout, 96" × 107¼"

2. Sew the triangle units by joining the blocks into rows, and then join the rows. Press all the seams open. Sew the 4 triangle units to the star center. Press the seams toward the star.

3. Sew the additional blocks into the number of rows indicated for your quilt size. Press the seams open. Sew the additional rows to the quilt.

4. Refer to Mitered Borders (page 24) to add the borders, using the black 1¾" (2½") strips as the first border and the main print 2¼" (4½") strips as the outer border.

5. Use your favorite methods to layer, quilt, and bind the quilt with the 2¼" strips.

Quilting details

THE GRAND FINALE:

DELIGHTFUL DIAMOND CHAIN

Made by Barbara Cline and and machine quilted by Patricia Bird

Finished quilt size: 96" × 107¼"

Note: Instructions for a 79½" × 102" quilt are given in parentheses.

Using *Midnight Star* (page 48) as the center, the classic diamond chain pattern was used to create this dramatic quilt.

Center is *Midnight Star* (project on page 48).

Since the inside finished star for this pattern is 46½″ × 46½″, the *Gradient Star*, *Blazing Star*, and *Garland Delight* projects cannot be used as a center in this *Delightful Diamond Chain* project. All the other star projects can be trimmed and used as a center for this project. *Delightful Diamond Chain* may appear complicated, but when broken down into 11¼″ × 11¼″ squares, it is challenging, but not as difficult as it may look. The graduation in the colors of the background fabrics gives the quilt depth, and the diamond chain running from corner to corner through each block makes it look challenging. The method used to make the diamond chain includes strip piecing.

Materials

This list gives only the yardage for the background blocks and borders. It does not include fabric for the center star. All yardage is based on 42″-wide fabric.

- **Red solid:** ½ (⅓) yard for the eight-pointed star

- **Red print 1:** ½ (⅓) yard for the eight-pointed star

- **Red print 2:** 1⅛ (¾) yards for the diamonds running through the quilt

- **Black:** 1½ (1⅓) yards for the background behind the eight-pointed star and the first border

- **Dark gray:** 1¼ (¾) yards for the second background

- **Medium-dark gray:** 1½ (⅞) yards for the third background

- **Medium gray:** 2 (1⅛) yards for the fourth background

- **Medium-light gray:** 2¾ (1⅝) yards for the fifth background

- **Light gray:** 3⅜ (2¼) yards for the background behind the diamond chain

- **Red/black print:** 1⅔ (1½) yards for the second border

- **Backing:** 8⅔ (7¼) yards

- **Binding:** ⅞ (¾) yard

- **Batting:** 104″ × 115″ (87″ × 110″)

- **Template plastic**

Cutting

The numbers in parentheses are for the 79½″ × 102″ quilt. The Delightful Diamond Chain *template patterns are on pages 92–93. Label all the pieces.*

Red solid:

- Cut A2—7 (4) strips 1⅝″ × WOF*; subcut 1⅝″ diamonds for a total of 108 (60).

Red print 1:

- Cut A1—7 (4) strips 1⅝″ × WOF*; subcut 1⅝″ diamonds for a total of 108 (60).

Red print 2:

■ Cut diamond chain—20 (12) strips 1¾″ × WOF*.

Black:

■ Cut B—8 (5) strips 3½″ × WOF*; subcut 81 (45) squares 3½″ × 3½″, and cut diagonally twice for a total of 324 (180) triangles.

■ Cut first border—12 (10) strips 1¾″ (2½″) × WOF*.

Dark gray:

■ Cut C—22 (12) strips 1⅝″ × WOF*; subcut pieces with template C for a total of 108 (60).

Medium-dark gray:

■ Cut D—27 (15) strips 1⅝″ × WOF*; subcut pieces with template D for a total of 108 (60).

Medium gray:

■ Cut E—36 (20) strips 1⅝″ × WOF*; subcut pieces with template E for a total of 108 (60).

Medium-light gray:

■ Cut F—54 (30) strips 1⅝″ × WOF*; subcut pieces with template F for a total of 108 (60).

Light gray:

■ Cut G—6 (4) strips 3″ × WOF*; subcut pieces 2″ × 3″ for a total of 120 (72).

■ Cut H—1 (1) strip 3″ × WOF*; subcut 4 squares 3″ × 3″, and cut diagonally once for a total of 8 (8) triangles.

■ Cut diamond chain—40 (24) strips 2″ × WOF*.

Red/black print:

■ Cut second border—8 (8) strips 2¼″ (4½″) × length of fabric.

Binding:

■ Cut 11 (10) strips 2¼″ × WOF*.

WOF = width of fabric

Making the Diamond Chains

1. Follow the instructions for strip sets (page 18). For the diamond chain, sew a red 1¾″ strip between light gray 2″ strips as shown. Press the seams toward the red. Make 20 (12) strip sets. Then cut 1¾″ sections as shown. Use all the strip sets. Cut 300 (180) sections.

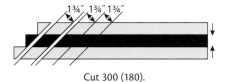

Cut 300 (180).

2. Sew 5 sections from Step 1 together to make a diamond chain, matching and pinning each seam as shown.

Make 60 (36) sections.

3. Sew a light gray G piece to each end of each diamond chain, centering the G piece on the last diamond as shown. Press the seam toward G. Complete 60 (36).

4. Use a see-through ruler and rotary cutter to trim the diamond chains ¼″ from the side diamond tips on both sides as shown.

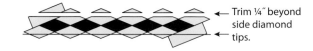

← Trim ¼″ beyond side diamond tips.

5. Use a see-through square ruler and a rotary cutter to trim off the ends of the diamond chains. Trim at 45° from the end diamond tips.

Trim off fabric at 45° angle ¼″ from diamond end tip.

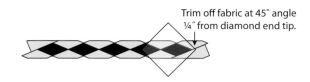

Making the Blocks

MAKING THE SMALL DIAMOND UNITS

Arrange an A1, an A2, and 3 B pieces to form a corner unit for the block. Refer to Y-seams (page 19) to sew the unit together. Complete the Y-seam before adding the end B pieces.

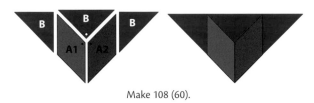

Make 108 (60).

COMPLETING THE BLOCKS

1. Sew pieces C, D, E, F, and a small diamond unit together as shown. Make 108 (60). Press the seams away from the small diamond unit.

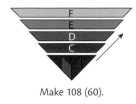

Make 108 (60).

2. Use a pin to mark the center of the long edge of each unit from Step 1, and match it to the center diamond in the diamond chain unit. Sew a diamond chain between 2 units from Step 1. Make 48 (24). Press the seams away from the diamond chain.

Make 48 (24).

MAKING THE HALF-BLOCKS

Use the remaining units from Step 1, and add a diamond chain to each one as shown. Make 12 (12). Press the seam away from the diamond chain.

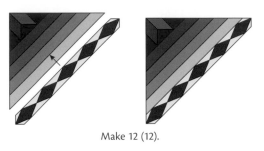

Make 12 (12).

Assembling the Quilt Top

1. Arrange 3 blocks and 3 half-blocks with 2 H pieces as shown. The H piece is sewn as part of row 2 and part of row 3. Sew each row together. Press the seams open. Join the rows to make the triangle unit. Make 4 (4).

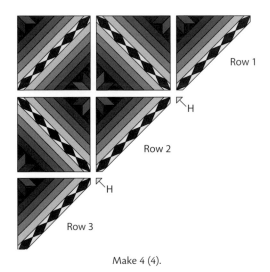

Row 1

Row 2

Row 3

Make 4 (4).

2. After pressing the seams open, the H piece will extend beyond the fabric edges. Trim the edges even with each triangle unit.

3. Trim the star quilt center to 47" × 47".

4. Arrange the triangle units around the star center. Because the star center has the diamond border added with the half-blocks, each side of the center has a Y-seam with the triangle units and the center. Refer to Y-seams (page 19) to sew the triangle units to the center.

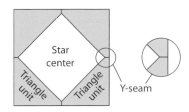

5. Refer to the quilt layout for the 96″ × 107¼″ quilt to arrange the blocks around the center from Step 4. If you are making the 79½″ × 102″ quilt, you will not add the second row to the bottom of the quilt, and you will not add the side rows of blocks. Arrange the blocks for the additional rows. Check the color placement throughout the quilt.

Quilt layout, 96″ × 107¼″

6. Sew the additional blocks into the number of rows indicated for your quilt size. Press the seams open. Sew the additional rows to the quilt.

7. Refer to Mitered Borders (page 24) to add the borders, using the black 1¾″ (2½″) strips as the first border and the red/black print 2¼″ (4½″) strips as the outer border.

8. Use your favorite methods to layer, quilt, and bind the quilt with the 2¼″ strips.

Quilting detail

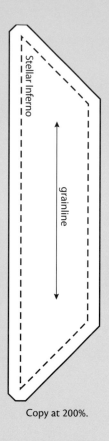

Stellar Inferno

grainline

Copy at 200%.

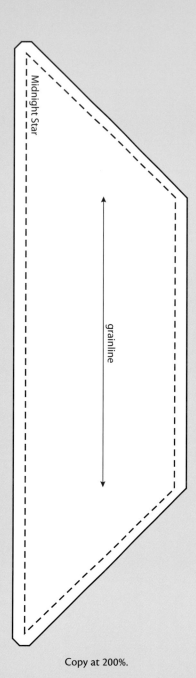

Midnight Star

grainline

Copy at 200%.

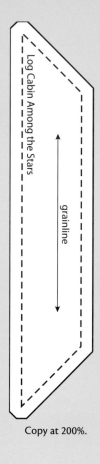

Log Cabin Among the Stars

grainline

Copy at 200%.

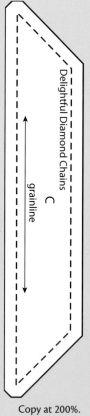

Delightful Diamond Chains

C

grainline

Copy at 200%.

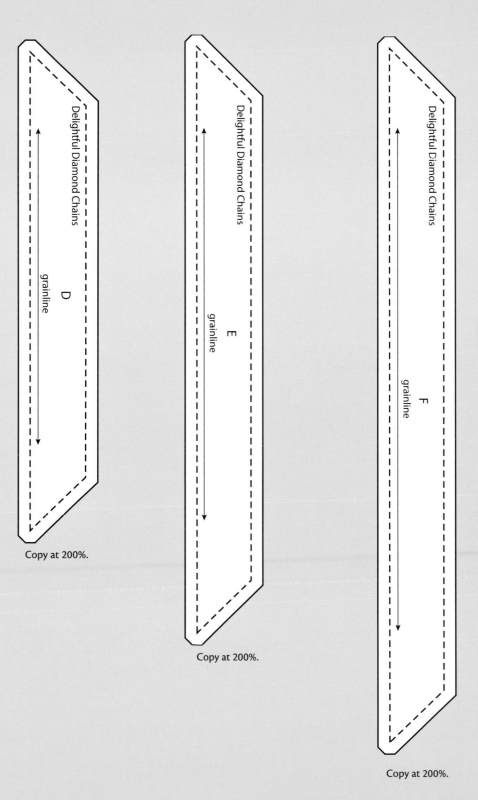

Delightful Diamond Chains

D

grainline

Copy at 200%.

Delightful Diamond Chains

E

grainline

Copy at 200%.

Delightful Diamond Chains

F

grainline

Copy at 200%.

RESOURCES

Best Press Spray Starch

Mary Ellen Products, Inc.
www.maryellenproducts.com

HeatnBond Lite

Therm O Web
www.thermowebonline.com

Pen Style Chaco Liner, Flower Head pins

Clover
www.clover-usa.com

Perfect Piecer

Jinny Beyer
www.jinnybeyer.com
This tool has different angles to mark the ¼" dots.

Retayne color fixative

G&K Craft Industries, Ltd.
www.gkcraft.com
Also available from www.dharmatrading.com.

Note: Most of these and many other useful supplies and notions are also available at your local quilt shop.